STECK-VAUGHN

MAPS • GLOBES • GRAPHS

Writer

Henry Billings

Consultants

Gloria Sesso
Dix Hills, New York

Edna Whitfield
St. Louis, Missouri

STECK-VAUGHN
ELEMENTARY · SECONDARY · ADULT · LIBRARY

A Harcourt Company

www.steck-vaughn.com

Acknowledgments

Editorial Director	Diane Schnell
Project Editor	Janet Jerzycki
Design Manager	Rusty Kaim
Electronic Production	UG/GGS Information Services, Inc.
Media Researcher	Claudette Landry
Cover Design	Donna Neal
Cartography	Land Registration and Information Service Amherst, Nova Scotia, Canada
	Gary J. Robinson
	MapQuest.com, Inc.
	R.R. Donnelley and Sons Company

Photography Credits

COVER (globe, clouds): © PhotoDisc; p. 4 © Patti McConville/The Image Bank; p. 5 (t) © PhotoDisc; p. 5 (b) © Rob Crandall/Stock Boston; pp. 6 (both), 7 (both) © PhotoDisc; p. 8 © Gordon R. Gainer/The Stock Market; p. 15 © Cenzus/FPG International; p. 75 (t) ©Aldo Brando/ Tony Stone Images; p. 75 (b) © Lena Rooraid/PhotoEdit.

Illustration Credits

Dennis Harms pp. 9, 15, 50, 51, 56 (both), 57 (both); Michael Krone pp. 29, 42; T.K. Riddle pp. 64, 68, 69; David Griffin pp. 65, 66, 67; Rusty Kaim p. 4

Contents

To The Learner

Maps•Globes•Graphs is a series of three books designed to help you learn the skills necessary for understanding and using maps, globes, and graphs. Since you will be working with maps directly on each page, you will get lots of hands-on experience. You should find this experience helpful when you read road maps, atlases, and a variety of the kinds of charts and graphs you find in newspapers and magazines.

Each of the chapters in this book focuses on one skill. In Book 1 the first eight chapters deal with map and globe skills. The last chapter focuses on skills needed to read bar graphs, circle graphs, line graphs, time lines and flow charts.

In addition to the chapters, you will find a few other features in this book. On pages 76–78 are atlas maps of the United States and the world. You may find these as well as the glossary on pages 79 and 80 handy references. On pages 81–84 there is a sample standardized test. This test covers many of the skills in the book. Its main purpose is to familiarize you with a standardized test format. If you are a student, you will probably take a test similar to this one some time in the future. The answer key is on pages 85–89. The answer key provides the answers to all of the questions in this book. Following the answer key are several outline maps that you can use to practice the skills you learn in the chapter.

As you work through this book, you will take a trip around the world. Enjoy your trip!

Geography Themes

In *Maps•Globes•Graphs* you will learn about some of the tools that scientists use to study **geography**. Geography is the study of Earth and the ways people live and work on Earth. Scientists use five themes, or main ideas, to help them organize information as they study geography.

The Five Themes of Geography
- **Location**
- **Place**
- **Human/Environment Interaction**
- **Movement**
- **Regions**

Location

Location is where something can be found. One way to describe the location of something is by using numbers and a street name, or an address. Another way is by telling what the location is near.

Think about your home. Where is it located? What it is near? Think about the numbers and street name that make up your address.

 This picture shows part of a crowded city. What makes it possible for mail to get to the right home or business?

Place

Place describes a location. Place tells about the **physical features** formed by nature, such as bodies of water, landforms, climate, and **natural resources**. Natural resources are things from nature that people can use. Some natural resources are trees, oil, and gold. Place also tells about the location's **human features**, or features made by people. Some examples of human features are buildings, roads, farms, schools and shopping malls.

This picture shows Baltimore, Maryland. Look for physical and human features of Baltimore in the picture. Describe three features of Baltimore.

_____

_____

 Think about the features of your town or city. Describe three features of your town or city. Tell if they are physical or human features.

_____

_____

Human/Environment Interaction

Human/Environment Interaction describes how people live with their **environment**, or surroundings. The landforms, natural resources, and climate often determine how people live. For example, the kinds of food people eat often depends on their environment and what can grow there. Also, the houses people build and the jobs that they do often depend on the environment.

 How are the people who live in this house able to live at the edge of the ocean?

_____

_____

_____

Human/Environment Interaction also describes how people live in their environment by changing it. People might cut down trees to clear the land and build offices and other buildings.

 Look at the pictures shown here. Why have people changed the environment in these places?

_____

_____

_____

_____

Movement

Movement describes how people, goods, information, and ideas move from place to place. Movement happens through transportation and communication.

People move in cars, buses, ships, trains, and planes. What are some ways goods move from place to place?

Information and ideas also move from place to place. This happens in newspapers, magazines, by telephone, and on radio and television.

Describe the kind of movement taking place in this picture.

_____

Regions

Regions are areas that share one or more features. A physical feature can describe a region. The Ohio River Valley is a physical landform region described by the Ohio River. Also, a human feature, such as how the land is used, can describe a region. Coal mining areas, such as those found in West Virginia and Kentucky form human land use regions because the land is used to mine natural resources. Regions can be as large as your state or as small as your neighborhood.

 The Rocky Mountains run through Canada and the United States for more than 3,000 miles. What do you think makes the Rocky Mountains a region?

_____

_____

_____

_____

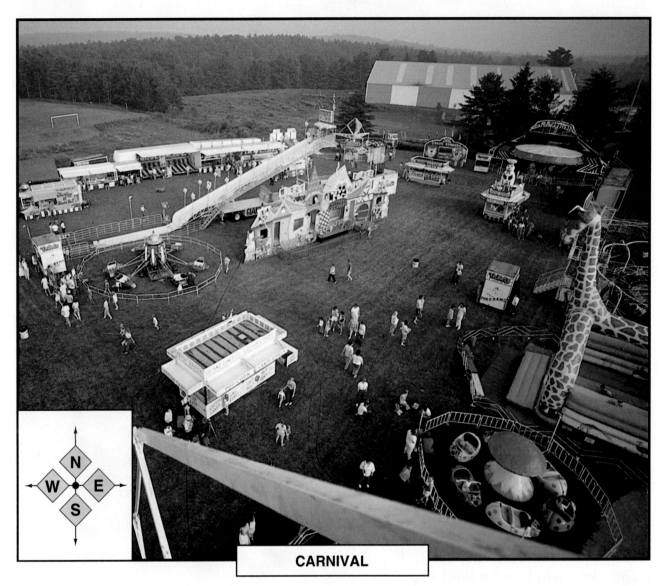

CARNIVAL

Look at the photograph shown here. The **title** of the photograph tells you what you are looking at. The title has large dark print.

A **compass rose** helps you find directions. Find the compass rose at the bottom of the photograph. A compass rose always tells you which way is north (N). Find the arrows pointing to south (S), east (E), and west (W). These are four **cardinal directions.**

► In which direction on the photograph do you look to find the giraffe bounce?

► In which direction on the photograph do you look to find the slide?

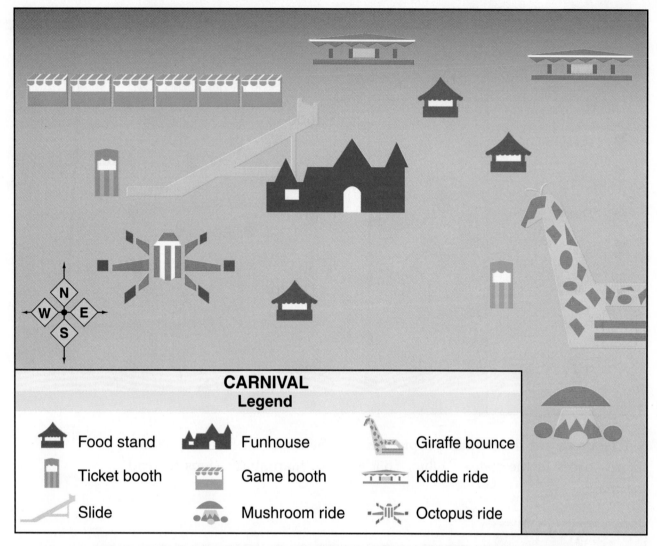

CARNIVAL
Legend

Food stand		Funhouse		Giraffe bounce	
Ticket booth		Game booth		Kiddie ride	
Slide		Mushroom ride		Octopus ride	

This is a **map** of the photograph on page 8. A map is a drawing of a real place. On a map **symbols** stand for real things. To know what map symbols mean, you need to read the **map key** or **legend**. Find the symbol for funhouse in the legend and locate it on the map. Can you find the funhouse in the photograph on page 8?

► Compare the photograph and the map. What do you see in both the photograph and the map?

► Is there anything in the photograph that is not on the map?

► Why do you think some things are not on the map?

Most maps have a compass rose to show directions. Find the compass rose on this map.

► What direction is it from the giraffe bounce to the octopus ride?

► What direction is it from the mushroom ride to the giraffe bounce?

► What direction do you walk if you go from the game booths to the slide?

Reading a Resource Map

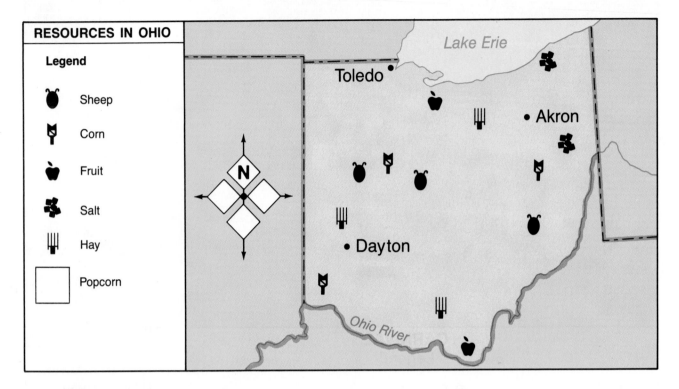

Resources are things that people can use. Symbols on this map stand for resources in the state of Ohio. Follow these map attack steps to read the map.

MAP ATTACK!

- **Read the title.** This map shows _____.
- **Read the legend.** Check (✔) each symbol as you read its meaning. Then check (✔) a matching symbol on the map.
- **Read the compass rose.** Circle the north arrow. Label the other three arrows.

1. Find a symbol for corn south of Akron. Circle it.
2. Find a symbol for hay north of Dayton. Circle it.
3. Find a symbol for sheep east of Dayton. Circle it.
4. Draw a symbol for popcorn in the legend where it belongs.
5. Draw two popcorn symbols. Draw one south of Toledo, and one west of Dayton.

6. What resource is found only in eastern Ohio? _____

7. What resource is found only in western Ohio? _____

Reading a Population Map

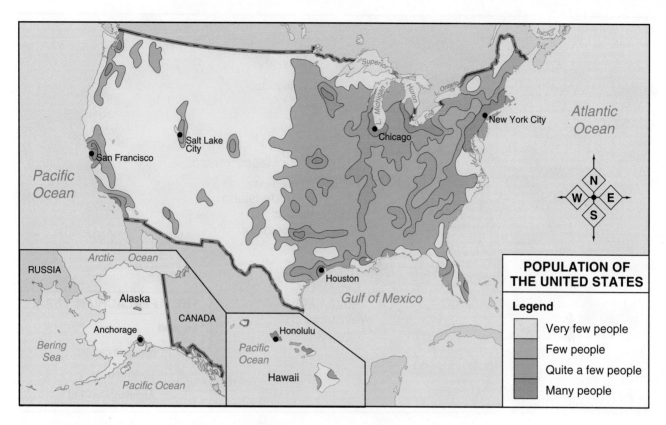

Population is the number of people who live in a place. Look at the population map above. It shows you how many people live in different areas of the United States.

1. Which color shows that many people live in an area?

   _____

2. Find the area where you live on the map. What color is your area?

   _____

3. Find Houston on the map. Do <u>many</u> or <u>very few</u> people live there?

   _____

4. Find Chicago on the map. Do <u>many</u> or <u>few</u> people live there?

   _____

5. Why do you think people want to live in these areas of our country?

   _____

Reading Symbols on a Map

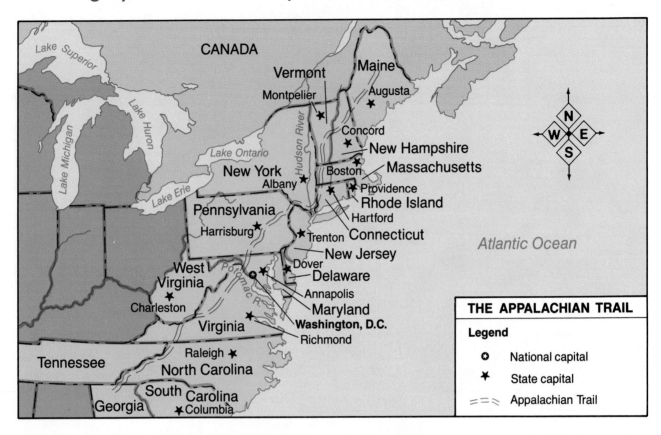

The Appalachian Trail is a hiking path in the eastern United States. It stretches through many different states. The Trail is over 2,000 miles long.

1. The northern end of the Appalachian Trail is in what state?

   _____

2. The southern end of the Appalachian Trail is in what state?

   _____

3. Which state capital is closest to the trail?

   _____

4. Which river crosses the Appalachian Trail and runs through our

   national capital? _____

5. Name two states that are completely east of the Appalachian Trail.

   _____ and _____

6. The trail crosses the Hudson River in what state?

   _____

✓ Skill Check

Word Check
      compass rose   symbol   cardinal directions
      map   legend   title

Write each word or phrase above in a sentence.

1. A _____ is a drawing of a real place.

2. A _____ stands for something real.

3. The _____ explains what the map's symbols mean.

4. The _____ helps you find directions on a map.

5. The letters N, S, E, and W stand for _____ .

Map Check

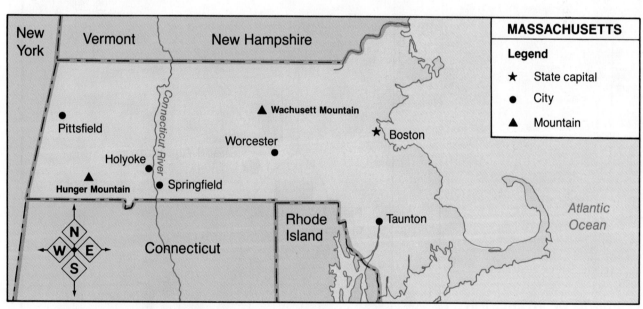

Find each place described below on the map. Write its name in the space provided.

1. A mountain west of Holyoke. _____

2. A city south of Wachusett Mountain. _____

3. A city along the eastern side of the Connecticut River.

_____

4. A city along the western side of the Connecticut River.

_____

Intermediate Directions

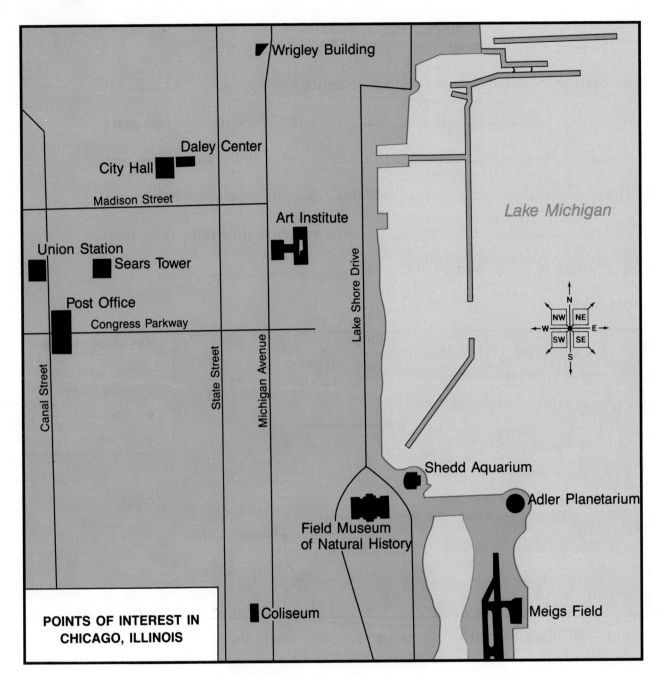

POINTS OF INTEREST IN
CHICAGO, ILLINOIS

You already know about the cardinal directions—north, south, east, and west. We use the cardinal directions to find places on Earth.

Look at the map above. Suppose you are at the Field Museum of Natural History in Chicago. Find it on the map. To get to the Adler Planetarium you go east.

You decide to walk from the Museum of Natural History to the Union Station. Find Union Station on the map. Are you walking north? Are you walking west? You are walking between north and west. That direction is called northwest.

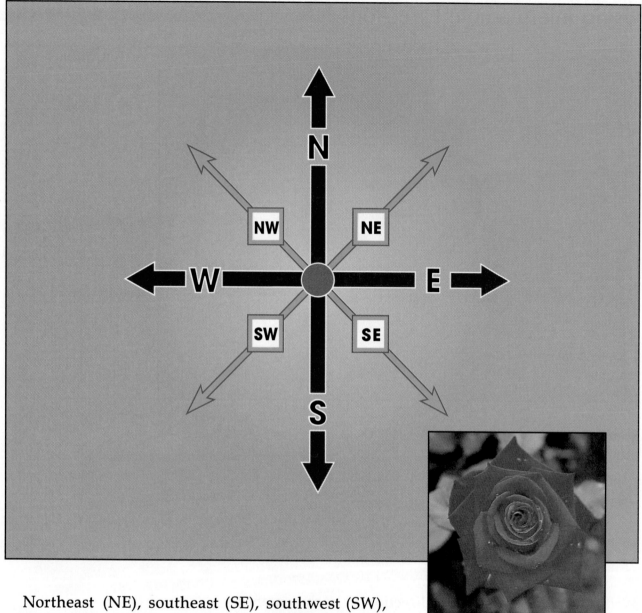

Northeast (NE), southeast (SE), southwest (SW), and northwest (NW) are **intermediate directions**. Look at the compass rose above. Find the arrows for north, east, south, and west. Then find the "in-between" arrows. These arrows point to the intermediate directions. Notice how the compass rose looks like an unfolding flower.

You can practice finding intermediate directions every time you read a compass rose. Practice now on the map on page 14.

▶ From the Field Museum of Natural History, which direction is each of these places?

        Coliseum   Meigs Field   Sears Tower

▶ Find City Hall on the map. Which direction would you walk to get to each of these places?

        Union Station   Art Institute   Wrigley Building

Using Intermediate Directions

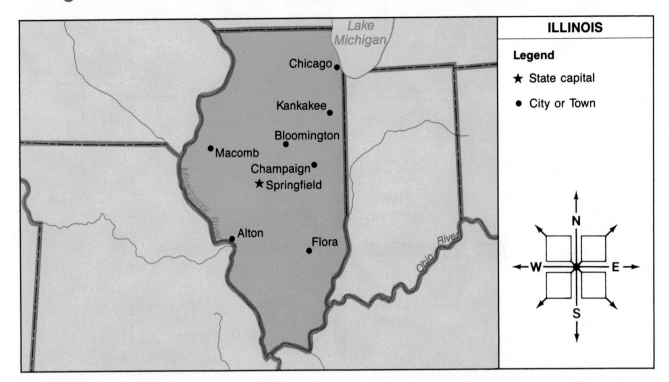

MAP ATTACK!

- **Read the title.** This map shows _____.
- **Read the compass rose.** Label the intermediate direction arrows. Use NE for northeast, SE for southeast, SW for southwest, and NW for northwest.

Write the best intermediate direction in each sentence.

1. Find Springfield, the capital of Illinois. Circle it.
   Draw a line from Springfield to Bloomington.

   Bloomington is _____ of Springfield.
2. Draw a line from Springfield to Alton.

   Alton is _____ of Springfield.
3. Draw a line from Springfield to Flora.

   Flora is _____ of Springfield.
4. Draw a line from Springfield to Macomb.

   Macomb is _____ of Springfield.

Using Intermediate Directions

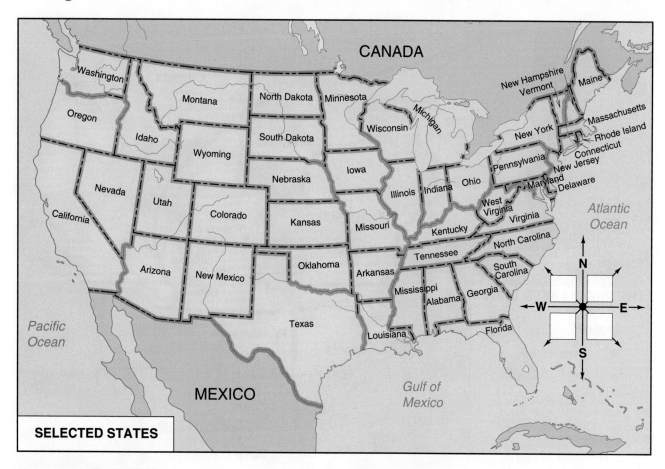

CANADA

Washington

Oregon

Idaho

Montana

North Dakota   Minnesota

South Dakota

Wyoming

Nevada

Utah

California

Colorado

Arizona   New Mexico

Nebraska

Iowa

Wisconsin

Michigan

Illinois Indiana   Ohio

New Hampshire
Vermont   Maine

New York   Massachusetts
                Rhode Island
Pennsylvania   Connecticut
            New Jersey
West   Maryland Delaware
Virginia
    Virginia   Atlantic
Kentucky   Ocean
    North Carolina

Kansas

Missouri

Oklahoma

Arkansas

Tennessee

Mississippi
    Alabama Georgia

South
Carolina

N
W   E
S

Pacific
Ocean

Texas

Louisiana

Florida

MEXICO

Gulf of
Mexico

SELECTED STATES

MAP ATTACK!

Follow the steps on page 16 to begin reading this map.

1. Find Colorado on the map. Circle the label.

   a. Which state is to the northeast of Colorado? _____

   b. Which state is to the southeast of Colorado? _____

   c. Which state is to the southwest of Colorado? _____

   d. Which state is to the northwest of Colorado? _____

2. Find each state below. In which part of the United States is it located?
   Write NE, SE, SW, or NW.

   a. Arizona _____   b. New York _____   c. Massachusetts _____

   d. Georgia _____   e. Oregon _____   f. South Carolina _____

   g. New Jersey _____   h. Florida _____   i. Pennsylvania _____

Directions in the Great Lakes States

1. Trace the state boundaries in green.
2. Trace the national boundary in red.
3. Color the states yellow.
   Choose another light color and color Canada.
4. Find each place below on the map. Write the direction you would travel from the first place to the second place. Use cardinal and intermediate directions. The first one is done for you.

a. Indianapolis to Columbus __E__

b. St. Paul to Madison _____

c. Lansing to Springfield _____

d. Grand Rapids to Ft. Wayne _____

e. Springfield to Madison _____

f. Ohio to Illinois _____

g. Wisconsin to Ohio _____

h. Lake Erie to Lake Superior _____

✓ Skill Check

Word Check   **intermediate**   **northwest**   **southwest**
                   southeast   **northeast**

1. Finish the compass rose on the map below. Add the intermediate directions NE, SE, SW, and NW.

2. _____ directions are between the cardinal directions.

Map Check

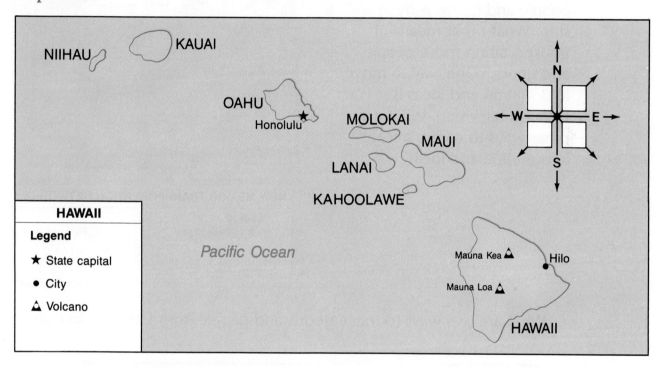

1. Find the island of Lanai on the map. Circle it.
2. Draw a line from Lanai to Maui.

   Maui is _____ of Lanai.
3. Draw a line from Lanai to the big island of Hawaii.

   Hawaii is _____ of Lanai.
4. Draw a line from Lanai to Oahu.

   Oahu is _____ of Lanai.
5. Find the city of Hilo on the big island of Hawaii.

   Which volcano is southwest of Hilo? _____

   Which volcano is northwest of Hilo? _____

Geography Themes Up Close

Movement tells how people, goods, information, and ideas move from place to place. Transportation and communication demonstrate movement. One way to move people and goods is by ship. What other means of transportation move people and goods? One way to move information and ideas is through television. What are other ways to communicate information and ideas?

NEW MEXICO TRANSPORTATION NETWORKS

Legend
★ State capital
• City
— Major highway
┼┼┼ Railroad
✕ Airport

1. What are two ways to move goods and people from Carlsbad to Clovis?

   _____

2. What city is the center of transportation in New Mexico? Why do you think this is so?

   _____

   _____

3. Trace the shortest driving route from Las Cruces to Santa Fe. What highway would you take from Las Cruces to Santa Fe?

   _____

4. What cities would you pass through between Las Cruces and Santa Fe?

   _____

5. New Mexico needs another airport. Put an **X** on the map where you think an airport should be built. Explain why you think this is a good location for an airport.

_____

_____

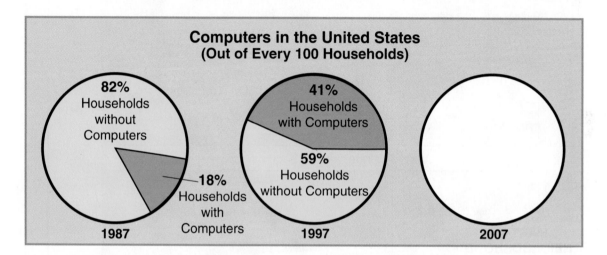

Computers in the United States
(Out of Every 100 Households)

82%
Households without Computers

18% Households with Computers

1987

41%
Households with Computers

59%
Households without Computers

1997

2007

Computers move information and ideas throughout the United States and the world. The first two circle graphs show the number of households (out of every 100 households) in the United States that have computers.

6. Out of every 100 households in 1987, how many had computers?

_____

7. Out of every 100 households in 1997, how many had computers? Is this number more or less than in 1987?

_____

8. Predict how many households out of every 100 in the United States will have a computer in 2007. Complete the circle graph for 2007 with the number you predict. Explain your prediction.

_____

_____

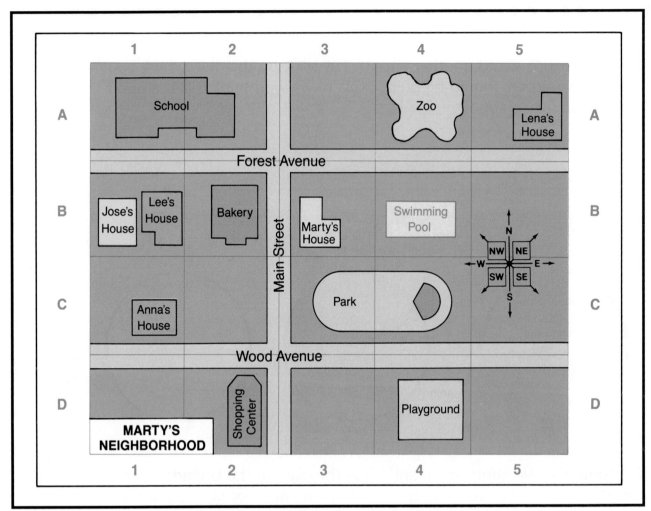

A **grid** is a pattern of lines drawn on a map to help you find places. We label the rows on a grid with letters. We label the columns with numbers. Find the letters along each side of the map above. Now find the numbers across the top and bottom. Do you see the squares on the map?

Locate Marty's house on the map above. It is in square B-3. Find the letter B on the left side of the map. Slide your finger across row B until you reach column 3. You are now in square B-3.

► Which building is located in the square to the west of B-3?
What is the name of this square?

► The zoo is located in square A-4. Find it on your map.
Where could you go if you walked south one square?
What is the name of this square?

► Anna rode her bike to the shopping center. It is in square D-2. Find it on your map. Later she will meet Marty at the bakery. The bakery is in square B-2.
Which direction should she bike to reach the bakery?

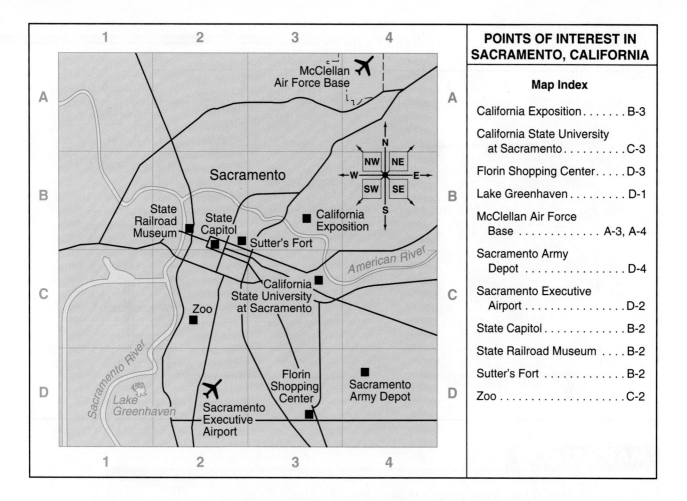

POINTS OF INTEREST IN
SACRAMENTO, CALIFORNIA

Map Index

California Exposition B-3

California State University
   at Sacramento C-3

Florin Shopping Center D-3

Lake Greenhaven D-1

McClellan Air Force
   Base A-3, A-4

Sacramento Army
   Depot D-4

Sacramento Executive
   Airport D-2

State Capitol B-2

State Railroad Museum B-2

Sutter's Fort B-2

Zoo C-2

You can find a place on a map grid by looking it up in the map index.
A **map index** is an alphabetical list of the places on the map. A map index
lists each place with the letter and number of its grid square.

Look at the map on this page. It shows places of interest in Sacramento,
California. To find places on the map, you use the map index. Suppose you
want to visit the zoo. Look up "zoo" in the map index. The map index tells
you that the zoo is in square C-2. To find this square on the map, put your
finger on the C and slide it across row C until you reach column 2. This is
square C-2. You can now find the zoo.

▶ Use the map index to find Lake Greenhaven. In which grid square is it
   located? Find Lake Greenhaven on the map.

▶ Look up Florin Shopping Center in the map index. In which grid square
   is it located? Find Florin Shopping Center on the map.

▶ Locate Sutter's Fort using the map index. In which grid square is it
   located? Find it on the map. Name two other points of interest located
   in this same square.

▶ Use the map index to find McClellan Air Force Base. Now find the
   Sacramento Army Depot. Which direction would you travel to get from
   McClellan Air Force Base to the Sacramento Army Depot?

Finding Places on a State Map

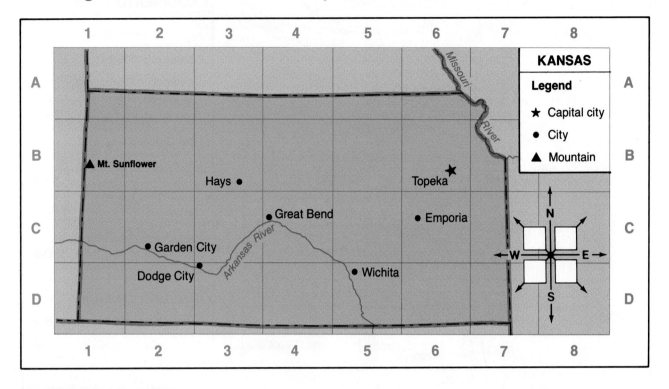

MAP ATTACK!

- **Read the title.** This map's title is _____.
- **Read the compass rose.** Label the intermediate direction arrows.

- **Read the grid.** There are ____ rows and ____ columns on the grid.

1. The capital city of Kansas is in square B-6.

   What is the name of this city? _____

2. The highest point in Kansas is in square B-1.

   What is the name of this mountain? _____

3. The largest city in Kansas is in square D-5.

   What is the name of this city? _____

4. Great Bend is a city in square C-4. Locate it on your map.

   This city is on which river? _____

5. Name two other cities on the Arkansas River. Then write the letter and number of their grid squares.

   _____

Finding Places on a Regional Map

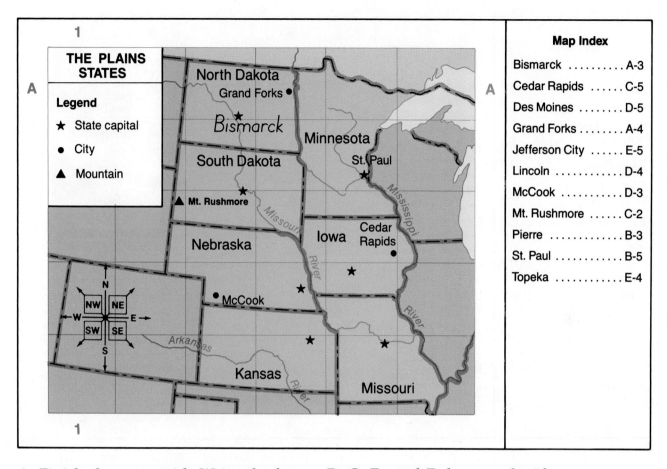

1. Finish the map grid. Write the letters B, C, D, and E down each side of the map. Write the numbers 2, 3, 4, 5, and 6 across the top and bottom of the map. The first letter and number are done for you.

2. Use the index to find the places listed below. Circle each one on the map. Then write the name of the state where each place is located.

   Mt. Rushmore _____   Cedar Rapids _____

   McCook _____   Grand Forks _____

3. Use the index to locate each state capital listed below. Write the name of each state capital where it belongs on the map. Then write the name of the state where each capital is located. The first one is done for you.

   Bismarck ___*North Dakota*___   Des Moines _____

   Jefferson City _____   Lincoln _____

   Pierre _____   Topeka _____

Finding Places in Yellowstone National Park

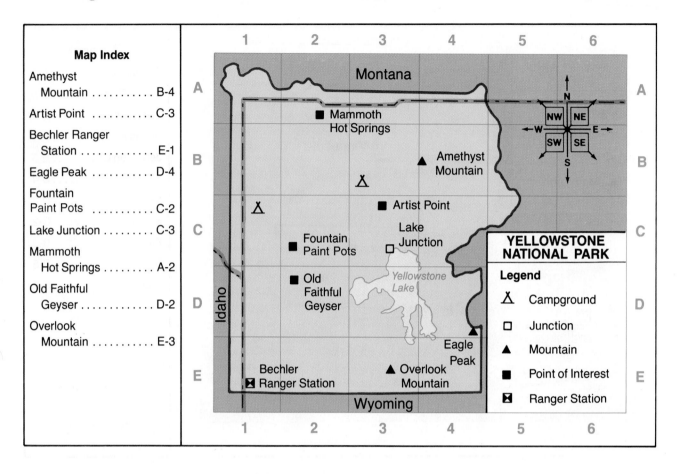

1. Use the map index to find each place on the map.
   Draw a circle around each place.

Old Faithful Geyser	Mammoth Hot Springs
Lake Junction	Fountain Paintpots
Bechler Ranger Station	Amethyst Mountain

2. Find Artist Point on the map. Draw a circle around it.
   Write the direction you would travel from Artist Point to each place
   below. The first one is done for you.

   Old Faithful Geyser __SW__   Yellowstone Lake _____

   Mammoth Hot Springs _____   Fountain Paintpots _____

   Amethyst Mountain _____   Bechler Ranger Station _____

3. Find the symbol for a campground in the legend.
   Draw a campground symbol southwest of Mammoth Hot Springs.

4. The highest mountain peak in Yellowstone Park is in square D-4.

   What is the name of this mountain? _____

Skill Check

Word Check   grid   index

1. A map _____ lists places found on a map. It is arranged in alphabetical order.

2. A _____ is a pattern of crossing lines that make rows and columns on a map.

Map Check

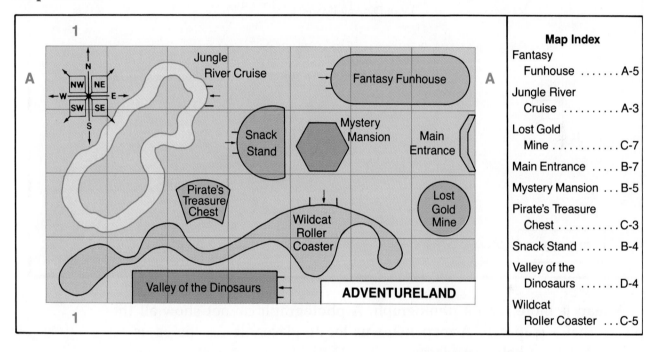

1. Finish the map grid. Label each row with a letter and each column with a number. The first ones are done for you.

2. Use the map index to find Mystery Mansion.

    In which square is it located? _____
    Find it on your map and draw a circle around it.

3. In which square is the Pirate's Treasure Chest located? _____
    Write the direction you would walk from Mystery Mansion to the

    Pirate's Treasure Chest. _____

4. In which square is the Lost Gold Mine located? _____
    Write the direction you would walk from Mystery Mansion to the

    Lost Gold Mine. _____

4 Distance and Scale

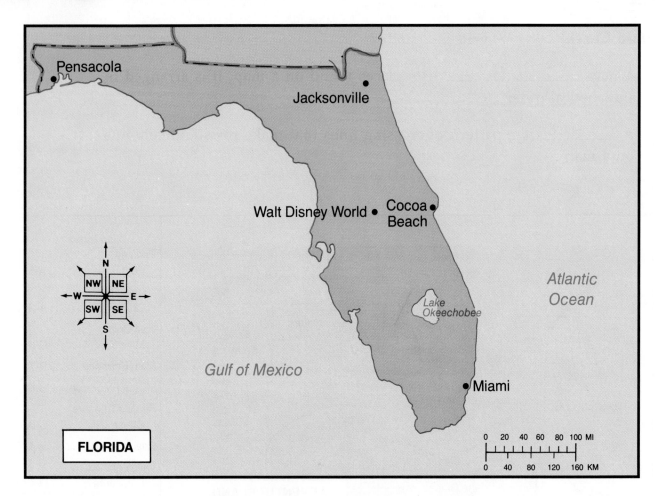

A map is more than a photograph. A photograph cannot show all the places that a map can. A map helps us locate places. It also helps us figure distances between places.

Florida is 450 miles long. A map cannot be that long! We must make maps small enough to hold. So on this map of Florida, one inch equals one hundred miles.

How do we know that? We find out that one inch equals one hundred miles by reading the **map scale**. A map scale looks like this:

The marks and numbers along the top stand for distance in miles. The marks and numbers along the bottom stand for distance in kilometers. **Miles** and **kilometers** are two ways of measuring distance.

▶ Find the map scale on the map above.
What letters stand for <u>miles</u>?
What letters stand for <u>kilometers</u>?

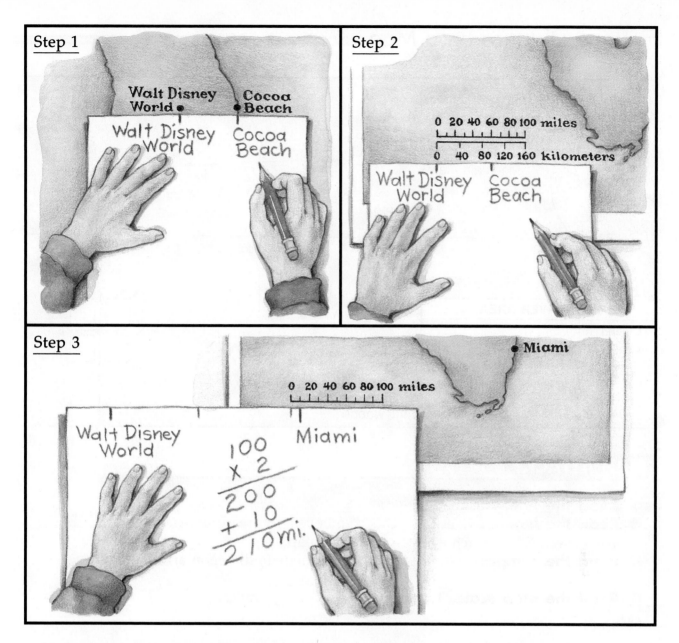

Step 1

Step 2

Step 3

You are on vacation in Florida. You want to find the distance between Walt Disney World and Cocoa Beach. Here's how you use the map scale.

Step 1 Place the edge of a piece of paper in a straight line from Walt Disney World to Cocoa Beach. Mark your paper below each city.

Step 2 Lay the edge of your paper along the scale. Your left-hand mark should be below "0". Read the scale numbers nearest your right-hand mark. The numbers tell you that Walt Disney World and Cocoa Beach are 60 miles apart.

Step 3 What if the distance is more than 100 miles? Find out how many times the scale fits between your two marks. Multiply the number of times it fits by the high number on the scale. Then add the extra amount.

► How many miles apart are Walt Disney World and Miami?

Figuring Distance on a Map

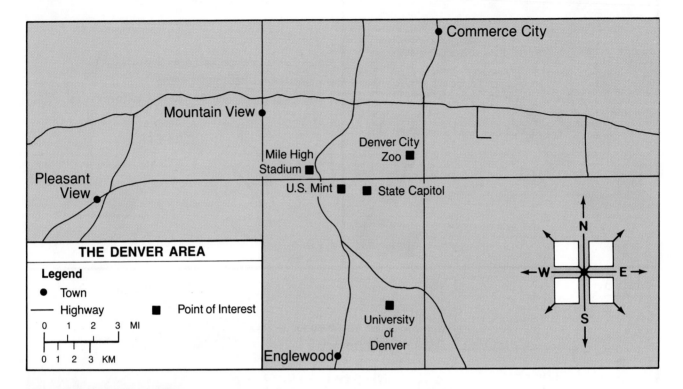

MAP ATTACK!

- **Read the title.** This map shows _____.
- **Read the legend.** Check (✔) each symbol as you read its meaning. Then check (✔) a matching symbol on the map.
- **Read the compass rose.** Label the intermediate direction arrows.

- **Read the map scale.** The scale goes up to _____ miles.

Use the map scale and the edge of a piece of paper to figure these distances. Write the distance in miles for questions 1 through 4. Write the distance in kilometers for question 5.

1. From the University of Denver to Mile High Stadium is about _____ miles.

2. From the Denver City Zoo to Englewood is about _____ miles.

3. From the State Capitol to the University of Denver is about _____ miles.

4. From the U.S. Mint to Commerce City is about _____ miles.

5. From Pleasant View to Mountain View is about _____ kilometers.

Figuring Distances on a Map

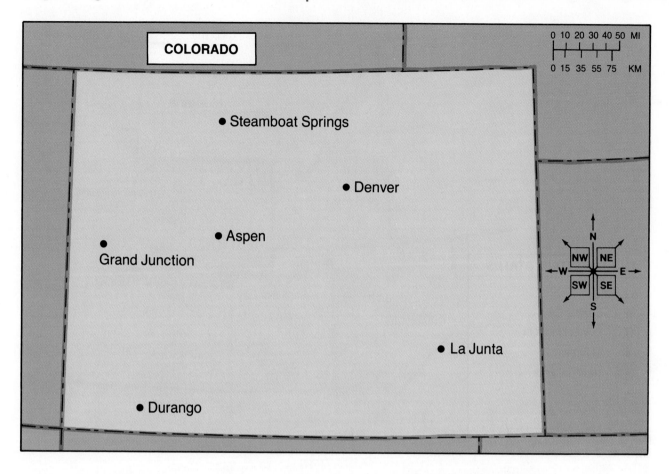

You are about to go on a flying trip through the Rocky Mountains. Your plane will land in several cities. How many miles will you travel?

Use the map scale and the edge of a piece of paper to figure the distance.

1. Draw a line from Denver to Durango.

   Measure the distance from Denver to Durango. _____ miles

2. Draw a line from Durango to Aspen.

   Measure the distance from Durango to Aspen. _____ miles

3. Draw a line from Aspen to Steamboat Springs.

   Measure the distance from Aspen to Steamboat Springs. _____ miles

4. Draw a line from Steamboat Springs to Denver.

   Measure the distance from Steamboat Springs to Denver. _____ miles

5. How many miles did you fly? Add the number of miles between each city. The total distance of your trip was _____ miles.

Figuring Distance in the Mountain States

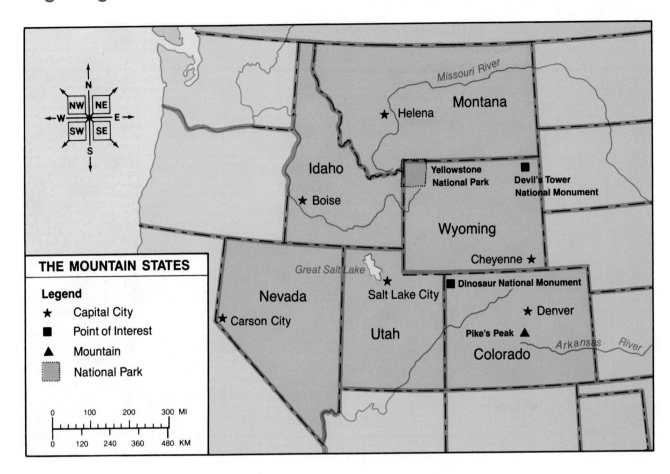

You and your family are planning a trip through the mountain states. Below is the daily log you need to complete before the trip. Finish the daily log. The first day is done for you.

Day 1 Drive from Yellowstone National Park to Devil's Tower.

Drive _____*east*_____ for about _____260_____ miles.

Day 2 Drive from Devil's Tower to Dinosaur National Monument.

Drive _____ for about _____ miles.

Day 3 Drive from Dinosaur National Monument to Pike's Peak.

Drive _____ for about _____ miles.

Day 4 Drive from Pike's Peak to Cheyenne.

Drive _____ for about _____ miles.

Day 5 Drive from Cheyenne to Yellowstone National Park.

Drive _____ for about _____ miles.

Skill Check

Word Check   **map scale**   **kilometers**   **miles**

Write each word in a sentence.

1. Two ways of measuring distance on Earth are _____

   and _____.

2. A _____ helps us measure distance on a map.

Map Check

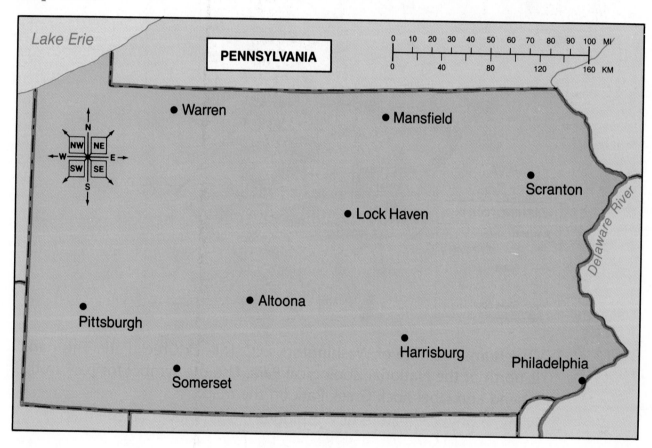

Use the map scale and a piece of paper to find these distances.

1. Somerset is about _____ miles from Altoona.

2. Mansfield is about _____ miles from Scranton.

3. Harrisburg is about _____ miles from Warren.

4. Altoona is about _____ miles from Pittsburgh.

Geography Themes Up Close

Place is a location that has physical and human features that make it different from any other location. Physical features can include natural resources, bodies of water, and plants and animals. Human features, those made by people, can include parks, playgrounds, buildings, bridges, railroads, and factories. The map below shows Washington, D.C. Look at the features that make Washington, D.C. different from any other place.

1. One human feature of Washington, D.C. is Rock Creek Park. This park is north of the National Zoological Park. Use the symbol for park in the legend and label Rock Creek Park on the map.

2. Name a physical feature of Washington, D.C. shown on the map.

_____

3. Find the U.S. Capitol on the map. It is southeast of the White House. Circle the U.S. Capitol. Write **P** next to it if it is a physical feature; write **H** if it is a human feature.

4. What are two other human features of Washington, D.C. shown on the map?

_____

5. Label the Colorado River on the map. Write **P** next to it if it is a physical feature; write **H** if it is a human feature.

6. What are two other physical features of the Grand Canyon?

_____

7. The Grand Canyon Village is a human feature of the Grand Canyon. It is in the southeastern part of the Grand Canyon. Circle the Grand Canyon Village.

8. What are two other human features of the Grand Canyon?

_____

9. Describe how the features of the Grand Canyon differ from the features of Washington, D.C.

_____

_____

_____

_____

5 🌐 Route Maps

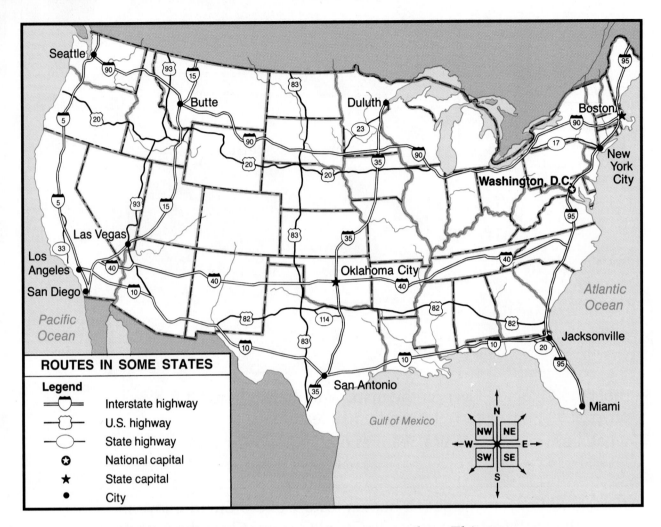

ROUTES IN SOME STATES

Legend
- Interstate highway
- U.S. highway
- State highway
- ✪ National capital
- ★ State capital
- ● City

A **route** is a way of getting from one place to another. This route map shows highways in the United States. The legend shows different highway symbols used on the map. Highways are named with numbers.

Three kinds of highways are shown on this map.

Interstate highway: a main highway with many lanes. Interstate highways often cross the entire country from east to west or from north to south.

U.S. highway: a main highway that passes through more than one state.

State highway: a main road that connects cities and towns within the boundaries of one state.

► Find each highway in the legend and on the map.

► What interstate highways run north and south on the map?

► What interstate highways run east and west on the map?

► What U.S. highways can you find on the map?

► What state highways can you find on the map?

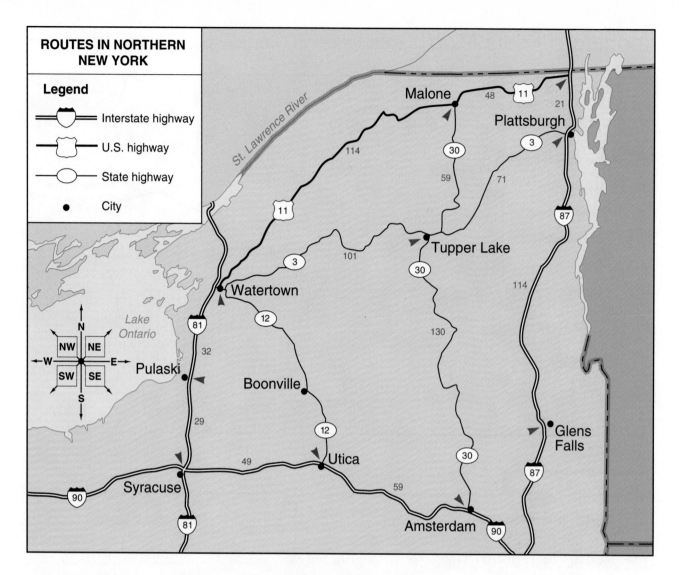

ROUTES IN NORTHERN NEW YORK

Legend

Interstate highway
U.S. highway
State highway
• City

Route maps can help you find the distances between places. Look at the map above. Find the cities of Syracuse and Utica. Do you see the small red triangles pointing to each city? Now find the red number 49 between the triangles. This number tells you that there are 49 miles between the triangles. You now know that Syracuse and Utica are 49 miles apart.

► How many miles apart are Utica and Amsterdam?

► How many miles apart are Amsterdam and Tupper Lake?

► How many miles apart are Plattsburgh and Glens Falls?

Sometimes you must add the red numbers to find out the total distance between places. Imagine that you are driving from Pulaski to Plattsburgh. To find out how far you will drive, answer these questions.

► How many miles is it from Pulaski to Watertown?

► How many miles is it from Watertown to Tupper Lake?

► How many miles is it from Tupper Lake to Plattsburgh?

► Now add up the numbers to find the distance from Pulaski to Plattsburgh.

Reading a Route Map

ROUTES IN CENTRAL MISSISSIPPI

Legend
- Interstate highway
- U.S. highway
- State highway
- State capital
- City

MAP ATTACK!

- **Read the title.** This map shows _____ .

- **Read the legend.** The three routes shown are _____

  _____ .

- **Read the compass rose.** Label the intermediate direction arrows.

1. What highway crosses the Mississippi River? _____

2. What highway enters Vicksburg from the north? _____

3. What U.S. highway goes through Jackson? _____

4. What other cities does that route go through? _____

   _____

5. Find the city where highways 16 and 35 meet.
   Label that city <u>Carthage</u>.

6. What U.S. highway goes alongside Interstate 55? _____

Reading a Route Map

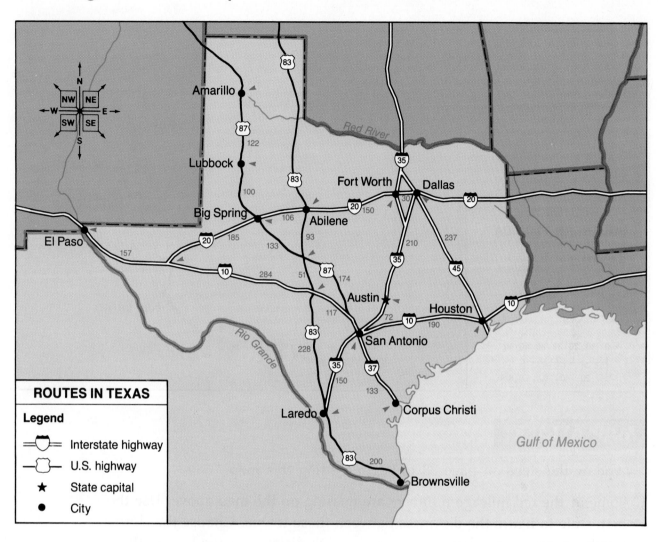

1. What does this map show? _____

2. Read the red mileage numbers between the cities below. Write the distances.

   Austin to San Antonio _____   Abilene to Fort Worth _____

   Laredo to Brownsville _____   Dallas to Houston _____

   Amarillo to Lubbock _____   San Antonio to Corpus Christi _____

3. Find the best route between each pair of cities below. Then add the red mileage numbers to figure the distance. Write the mileage.

   Corpus Christi to Dallas _____   Abilene to Brownsville _____

   El Paso to Fort Worth _____   San Antonio to El Paso _____

Reading a Route Map

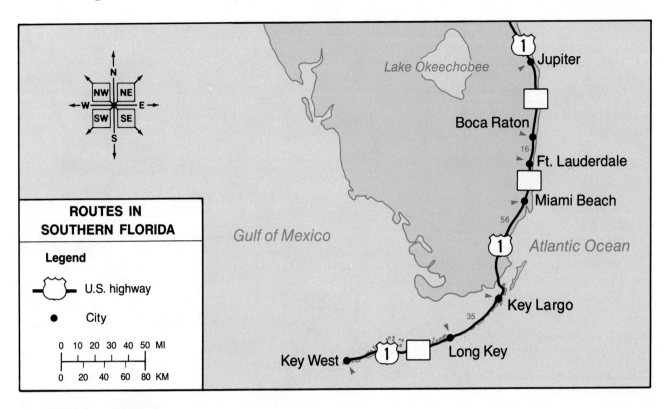

MAP ATTACK!

Follow the steps on page 38 to begin reading this map.

1. Some of the red mileage numbers are missing on the map above. Use the map scale to figure the distances between these towns. Choose the closest number from the box below. Then write each distance in the box on the map where it belongs.

   Key West to Long Key

   Jupiter to Boca Raton

   Ft. Lauderdale to Miami Beach

45	35
22	52
71	65

2. What is the distance between Key West and Key Largo? Use the mileage numbers from the map. _____

3. Find Jupiter on the map. Go south on U.S. Highway 1 for 139 miles.

   What city do you reach? _____

4. Continue south on U.S. Highway 1 to Key West. From Jupiter to

   Key West is _____ miles.

Skill Check

Word Check
        route   **U.S. highway**
        state highway   **interstate highway**

1. An _____ crosses the entire country.

2. A _____ connects cities and towns in one state.

3. A _____ passes through more than one state.

4. A _____ is a way of getting from one place to another.

Map Check

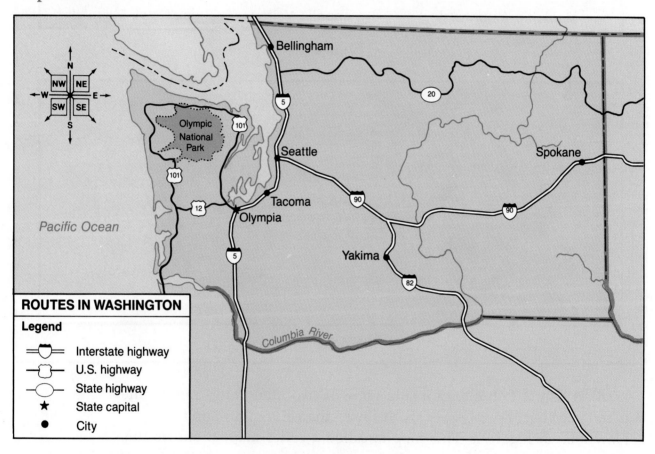

1. What interstate highway passes through Yakima? _____

2. Find Interstate Highway 5. What cities does it pass through?

   _____

3. What U.S. highway goes around Olympic National Park? _____

4. What state highway crosses the northern part of the state? _____

6 Relief Maps

Medicine Mountains   Pancake Valley   Black Hawk Mountains

Figure 1

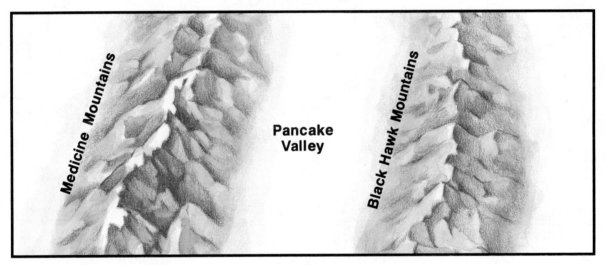

Medicine Mountains

Pancake Valley

Black Hawk Mountains

Figure 2

Look at Figure 1. It shows a side view of two mountains and a valley. You can see that the valley is much lower than the mountains.

Now look at Figure 2. This map is called a **relief map**. It shows the same mountains and valley. A relief map has shading to show where the land gets higher and lower. The higher mountains have darker shading. The lower mountains have light shading. The valley has no shading.

► Are the Medicine Mountains or the Black Hawk Mountains higher? How do you know?

► Which land is lower, the Black Hawk Mountains or Pancake Valley? How do you know?

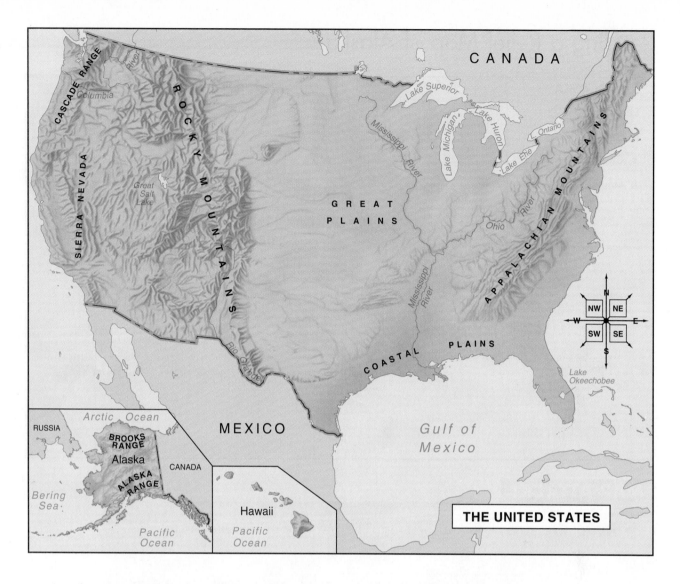

THE UNITED STATES

This is a relief map of the United States. On it are mountain ranges, plains, large lakes, and rivers. A **mountain range** is a chain, or group, of mountains. A **plain** is a large area of flat land. Find the Rocky Mountain range on the map. Now find the Great Plains on the map. Which area is darker?

On the map, the mountain ranges have dark shading. The higher the mountains, the darker the shading. The plains have little or no shading.

► Name the mountain ranges on the map.
  Where are they located?

► Which are higher, the Appalachian Mountains or the Rocky Mountains?
  How do you know this?

► Are there more mountains in the eastern or in the western United States?

► Find the Great Plains on the map.
  Name the mountain range west of the Great Plains.

Reading a Relief Map of Alaska

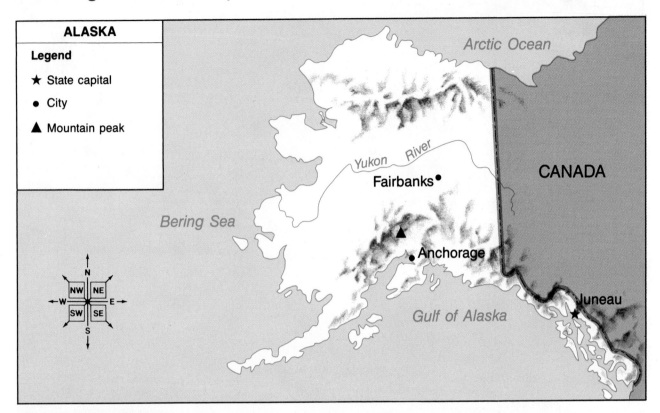

MAP ATTACK!

- **Read the title.** Look at the map. The purpose of this map is to

  show _____.
- **Read the legend.** Check (✔) each symbol in the legend. Check (✔) a matching symbol on the map.
- **Read the compass rose.** Circle the intermediate direction arrows.

1. Follow the directions below to finish the map.
   a. Write <u>Brooks Range</u> on the mountain range in northern Alaska.
   b. Write <u>Mt. McKinley</u> near the mountain peak between Anchorage and Fairbanks.
   c. Write <u>Coast Range</u> along the southern mountain range near Juneau.
   d. Write <u>Alaska Range</u> on the southern mountain range near Anchorage.

2. What river flows between the Brooks Range and the Alaska Range?

   _____

3. Does the Yukon River run through a valley or a mountain range?

   _____

Reading a Relief Map of the World

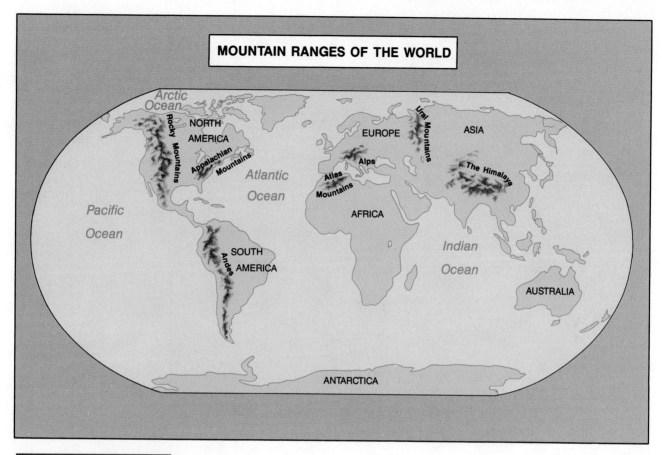

MOUNTAIN RANGES OF THE WORLD

MAP ATTACK!

Follow the first step on page 44 to begin reading this map.

1. Find the seven mountain ranges on the map. Circle the label for each range.

2. Complete this table. Find the continents listed below on the map. Write the name of a mountain range in each continent.

Continent	Mountain Range
North America	_____
South America	_____
Europe	_____
Asia	_____
Africa	_____

Reading a Relief Map of the Western United States

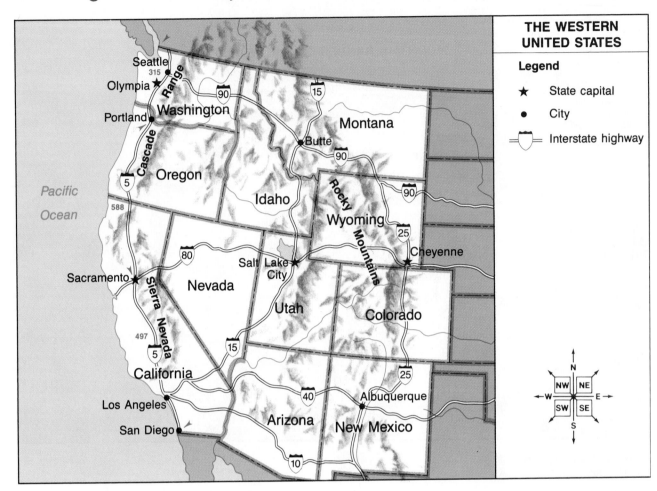

1. Locate Interstate 5 on the map. Trace it in red. This interstate runs along the western side of what two mountain ranges?

_____

2. How long is Interstate 5? Add the red mileage numbers to find the

   distance. Interstate 5 is _____ miles long.

3. Locate the Rocky Mountains on the map. Lightly color them green. What interstate runs along the western side of the Rocky Mountains?

_____

4. Find Cheyenne, Wyoming on your map. Circle it.

5. Find Interstate 80 going through Cheyenne. Trace Interstate 80 from Cheyenne to Sacramento.

6. What two mountain ranges does Interstate 80 cross?

_____

Skill Check

Word Check   **relief map**   **mountain range**   **plain**

Write the word that best completes each sentence.

1. A _____ has shading to show where mountains and valleys are.

2. A _____ is a chain of mountains.

3. A _____ is a large flat area of land.

Map Check

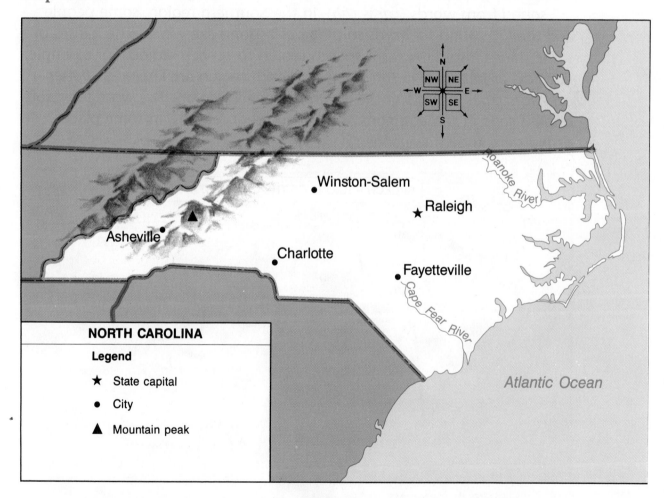

1. Follow the directions to label these places on the map.
   a. Write <u>Great Smoky Mountains</u> on the range west of Asheville.
   b. Write <u>Blue Ridge Mountains</u> on the range west of Winston-Salem.
   c. Write <u>Mt. Mitchell</u> on the mountain peak northeast of Asheville.

2. Are the mountains mostly in the east or in the west? _____

Geography Themes Up Close

Regions describe areas that have at least one feature that makes them different from other regions. Geographers organize areas into regions based on their physical features or their human features. For example, geographers might organize the United States into regions based on climate.

The map below shows speech regions in the United States. Most people in the United States speak English. But there are places in the United States where people have certain accents, or ways of pronouncing words. For example, in the New England speech region, people drop the "r" sound from words (*car* is *cah*). In the Southern region, some people add the "r" sound to words so that *wash* sound like *warsh*. The names of some things also differ from speech region to speech region. For example, *flapjacks* or *hot cakes* in the Western speech region are known as *batter cakes* or *crepes* in parts of the Southern speech region. The word for a soft drink is *soda* in some regions and *pop* in other regions. In some places *peanuts* are known as *goobers*.

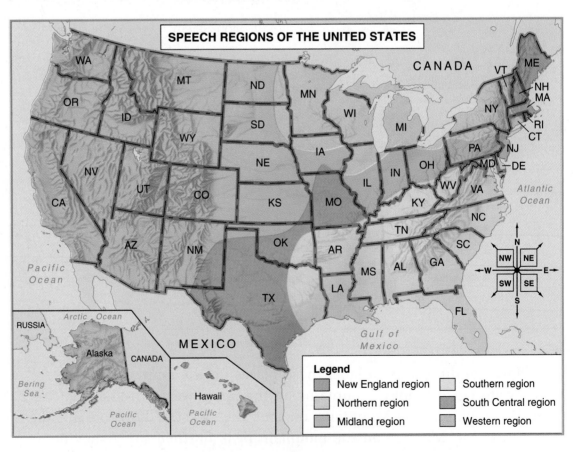

SPEECH REGIONS OF THE UNITED STATES

Legend
- New England region
- Northern region
- Midland region
- Southern region
- South Central region
- Western region

1. What kind of feature—physical or human—describes these regions?

   _____

2. According to the map, which speech region is the largest?

   _____

3. Find approximately where your community is located on the map. Mark it with an **X** on the map. In which speech region is your community?

   _____

4. In parts of Maine and New Hampshire, *pancakes* are called *griddle cakes*. These two states are part of which speech region?

   _____

5. In the Midland region, a *creek* is called a *crick* or a *run*. What states belong to the Midland region?

   _____

   _____

6. Differences in word pronunciation from one part of the country to another are not as noticeable today as they once were. Some differences are disappearing. Why do you think people in different parts of the United States are beginning to speak more alike?

   _____

   _____

   _____

   _____

   _____

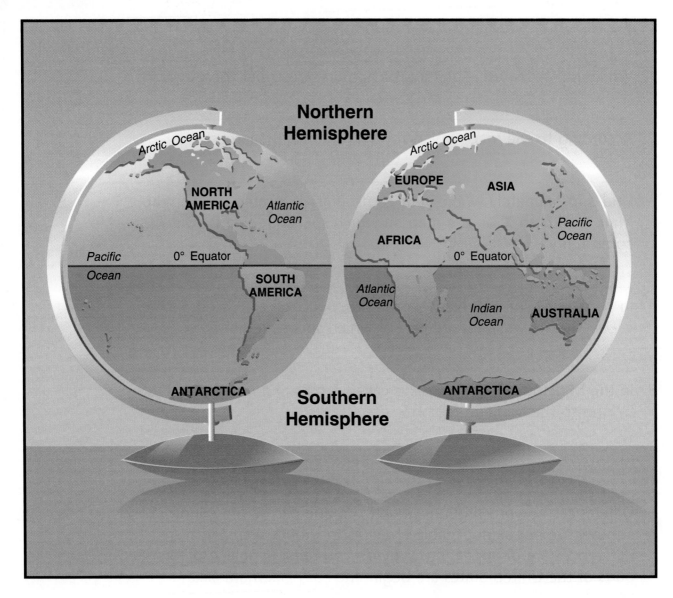

Study each side of the globe in the picture above. Find the dark line that circles the middle of the globe. That line is the **Equator**. The Equator is an imaginary line marked with zero. Find the zero marking the Equator.

The Equator divides the globe into two hemispheres. A **hemisphere** is half the globe. The half of the globe north of the Equator is the **Northern Hemisphere**. The half of the globe south of the Equator is the **Southern Hemisphere**.

▶ Find North America, Europe, and Asia in the Northern Hemisphere.

▶ Find Australia and Antarctica in the Southern Hemisphere.

▶ Trace the Equator with your finger.
   What continents and oceans does the Equator cross?

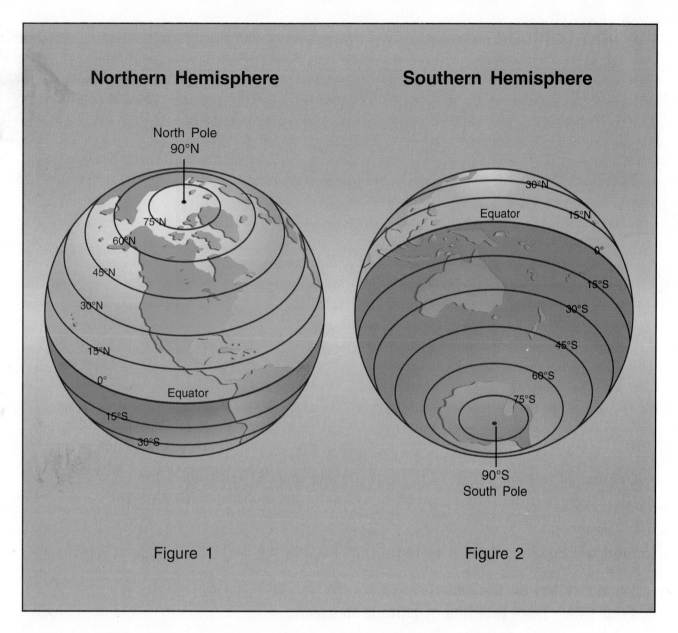

Northern Hemisphere   **Southern Hemisphere**

North Pole
90°N

75°N
60°N
45°N
30°N
15°N
0°
Equator
15°S
30°S

30°N
Equator
15°N
0°
15°S
30°S
45°S
60°S
75°S

90°S
South Pole

Figure 1   Figure 2

You can find places on globes and maps by using lines of **latitude**. The Equator is the most important line of latitude. The other lines of latitude measure distance north and south of the Equator.

All lines of latitude are numbered. Do you remember that the Equator is marked with a zero? It is 0° latitude. The sign ° stands for **degrees**. The lines that are farther away from the Equator have higher degree numbers. The North Pole is 90° north of the Equator. The South Pole is 90° south of the Equator. The North Pole and the South Pole have the highest degree numbers.

► Find 60° North latitude in Figure 1.
   What continents does it cross?

► Find 15° South latitude in Figure 2.
   What continent does it cross?

Finding Latitude

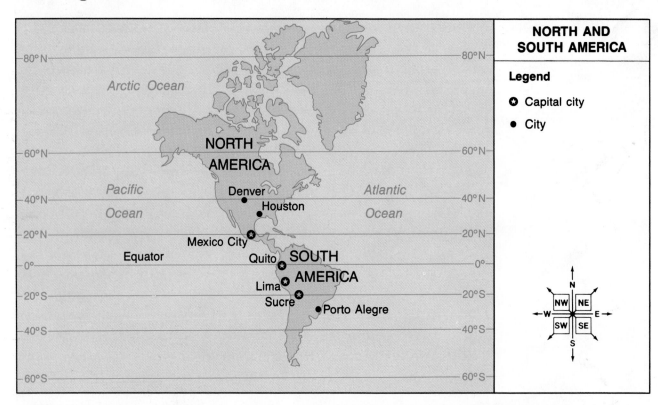

Degrees of latitude north of the Equator are marked with an N for north. Degrees of latitude south of the Equator are marked with an S for south.

1. Find the Equator. Trace it in red.

   What city lies on the Equator? _____

2. Find 20°N. Trace that line of latitude in green.

   What city lies at 20°N? _____

3. Find 20°S. Trace that line of latitude in orange.

   What city lies at 20°S? _____

4. Find 40°N. Trace that line of latitude in yellow.

   What city lies at 40°N? _____

5. Find Houston on the map. Circle it in green.
   Houston lies half way between 20°N and 40°N.

   Houston lies on what line of latitude? Make an estimate. _____

6. Find Lima on the map. Circle it in red.

   Lima lies on what line of latitude? Make an estimate. _____

Finding Latitude

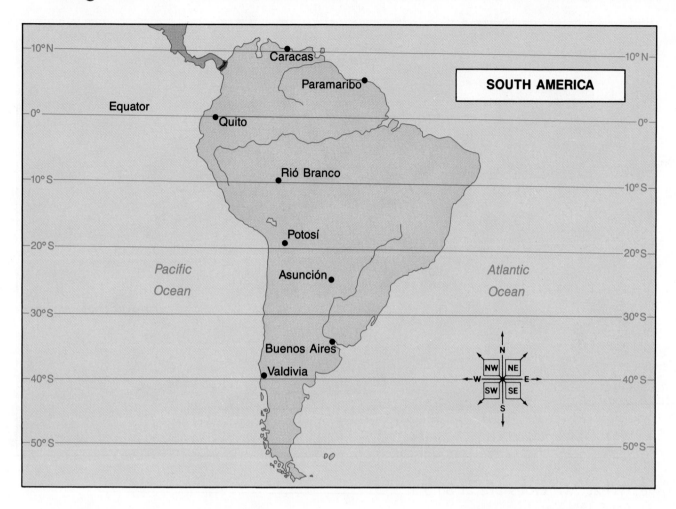

1. What city lies on the Equator? _____

2. What city lies near 20°S? _____

3. What city lies at 10°N? _____

4. What city lies at 40°S? _____

5. What city lies between 0° and 10°N? _____

   Estimate its line of latitude. _____

6. What city lies between 20°S and 30°S? _____

   Estimate its line of latitude. _____

7. What city lies between 30°S and 40°S? _____

   Estimate its line of latitude. _____

Finding Latitude

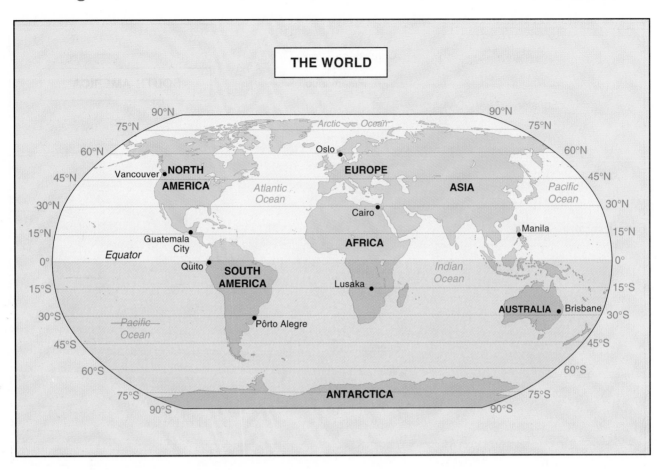

THE WORLD

1. What two cities are at 30°S? _____

2. What two cities are at 15°N? _____

3. What city is at 30°N? _____

4. What city is near 45°N? _____

5. What city is at 60°N? _____

6. What city is at 0°? _____

7. What city is at 15°S? _____

8. 75°S crosses which continent? _____

9. What direction would you go from Guatemala City to Oslo? _____

10. What direction would you go from Cairo to Pôrto Alegre? _____

11. What direction would you go from Manila to Oslo? _____

Skill Check

Word Check   latitude   Northern Hemisphere

                         Equator   Southern Hemisphere   degrees

1. The _____ is an imaginary line around the middle of Earth.

2. Lines of _____ measure distance north and south of the Equator.

3. Places north of the Equator are in the _____ .

4. Places south of the Equator are in the _____ .

5. Distances on a globe are measured in _____ .

Map Check

1. Find 1°S. What city lies near 1°S? _____

2. Find 1°N. What city lies at 1°N? _____

3. Find 4°S. What city lies at 4°S? _____

4. Find 2°S. What city lies near 2°S? _____

5. Find 3°S. What city lies near 3°S? _____

8 🌍 Longitude

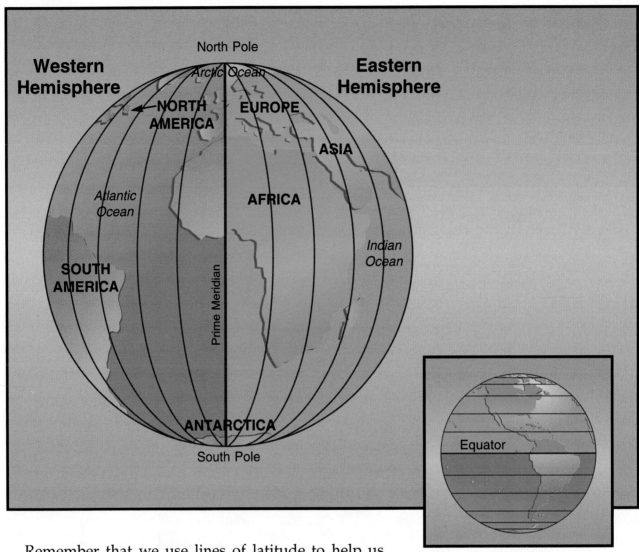

Remember that we use lines of latitude to help us
locate places on a globe or map. We also use lines of **longitude** to help us
locate places. Look at the large picture of a globe above. With your finger,
trace one line of longitude from the North Pole to the South Pole.

Look at the small picture of a globe. Notice that it has lines of latitude.

Remember that lines of latitude go around the globe. They don't touch.
Lines of longitude go only halfway around Earth, from the North Pole to the
South Pole. Lines of longitude all touch at each Pole.

Lines of longitude are numbered just like lines of latitude. The most
important line of longitude is the **Prime Meridian**. The Prime Meridian is
0° longitude.

▶ Trace the Prime Meridian with your finger.
  What continents does the Prime Meridian cross?
  What oceans does it cross?

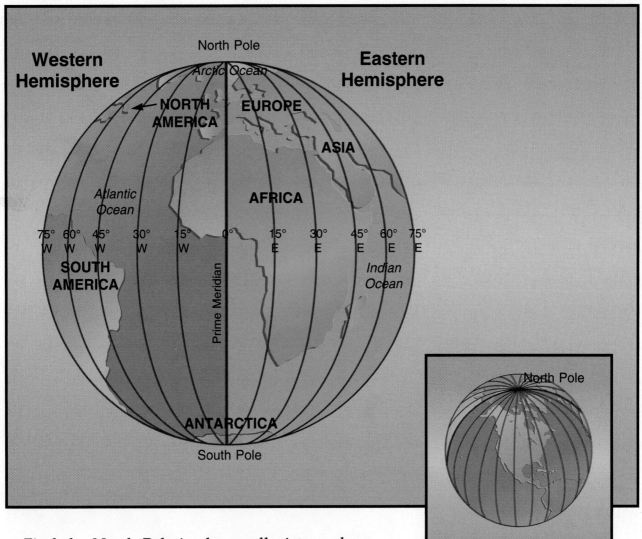

Find the North Pole in the small picture above.
Notice how all the lines of longitude meet at the North Pole. All the
lines of longitude meet at the South Pole too.

Lines of longitude are numbered up to 180°. The 180° line of longitude
and the Prime Meridian form a circle around the globe. That circle
divides the globe into the **Eastern Hemisphere** and the **Western
Hemisphere**. Find the Eastern and the Western Hemispheres in the large
picture above.

Lines of longitude in the Eastern Hemisphere measure distance east of
the Prime Meridian. Lines of longitude in the Western Hemisphere
measure distance west of the Prime Meridian.

► Find 15° West longitude in the large picture.
What continents does it cross?
What oceans does it cross?

► Find 30° East longitude.
What continents does it cross?

Finding Longitude

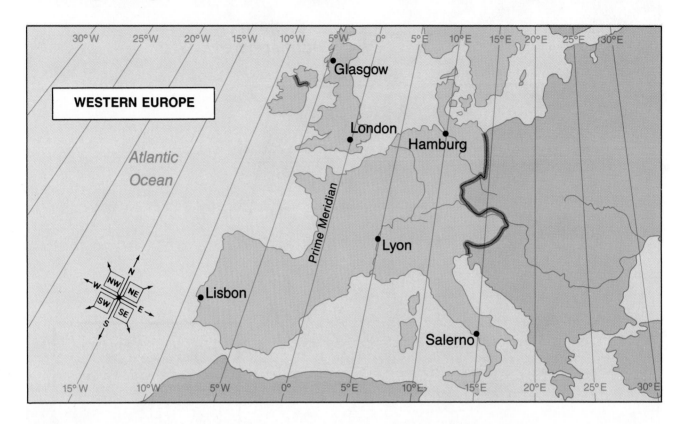

Degrees of longitude east of the Prime Meridian are marked with an *E* for east. Degrees of longitude west of the Prime Meridian are marked with a *W* for west.

1. Find the Prime Meridian. Trace it in red.

    What city lies on the Prime Meridian? _____

2. Find 5°W. Trace that line of longitude in green.

    What city lies near 5°W? _____

3. Find 5°E. Trace that line of longitude in orange.

    What city lies at 5°E? _____

4. Find 10°E. Trace that line of longitude in yellow.

    What city lies at 10°E? _____

5. Find 10°W. Trace that line of longitude in purple.

    What city lies near 10°W? _____

6. Find 15°E. Trace that line of longitude in brown.

    What city lies at 15°E? _____

Finding Longitude

1. What city lies on the Prime Meridian? _____

2. What city lies at 10°E? _____

3. What city lies near 10°W? _____

4. What city lies near 20°E? _____

5. What city lies near 30°E? _____

6. What city lies near 40°E? _____

7. What city lies near 50°E? _____

Finding Longitude

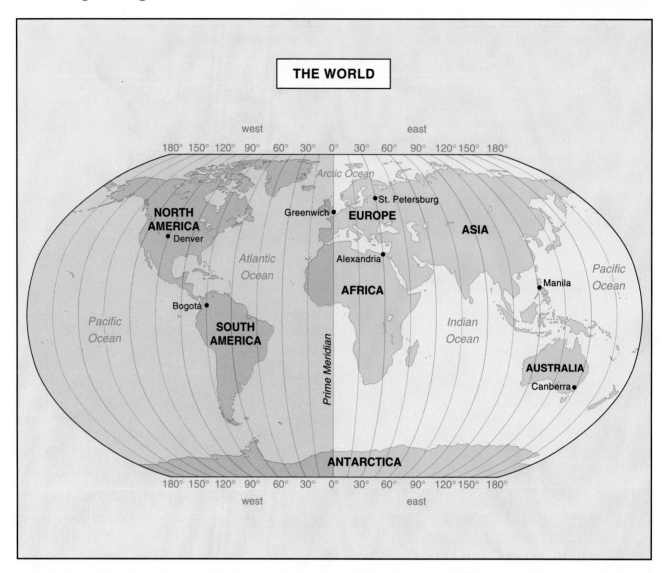

1. What two cities are at 30°E? _____

2. What city is at 105°W? _____

3. What city is near 120°E? _____

4. What city is at 150°E? _____

5. What city is at 75°W? _____

6. What city is on the Prime Meridian? _____

7. What direction would you go from Alexandria to Canberra? _____

8. What direction would you go from Bogotá to St. Petersburg? _____

Skill Check

Word Check   **longitude**   **Western Hemisphere**
                          Prime Meridian   **Eastern Hemisphere**

1. Lines of _____ measure distance east and west.

2. The _____ is at 0° longitude.

3. Places east of the Prime Meridian are in the _____ .

4. Places west of the Prime Meridian are in the _____ .

Map Check

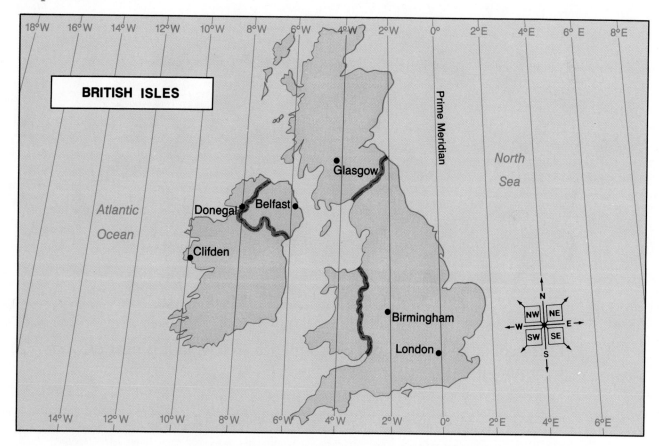

1. Find 2°W. What city lies at 2°W? _____

2. Find 0°. What city lies at 0°? _____

3. Find 6°W. What city lies near 6°W? _____

4. Find 4°W. What city lies near 4°W? _____

5. Find 10°W. What city lies at 10°W? _____

Geography Themes Up Close

Location describes where places are found. Every place on Earth has a location. There are two ways of describing a location. You can describe location by telling what it is near or what is around it. You can say that the Indian Ocean is south of Asia, east of Africa, and west of Australia. You also can describe location by its exact position on Earth by using a grid. Lines of latitude and longitude cross one another. This forms a grid on maps and globes to give the exact location of a place. If you know the latitude and longitude of a place, you can find it on a map or a globe.

1. Describe the location of North America. Tell what it is near or what is around it.

   _____

   _____

2. Notice on the map that Cairo and New Orleans are located on the same line of latitude—30°N. Find these two cities on the map. Circle them.

3. Cairo and New Orleans, however, are not located at the same place because they are located on different lines of longitude. To give the exact location of a place, you must give both the latitude and the longitude. We say that the exact location of Cairo is 30°N, 30°E. What is the exact location of New Orleans?

_____

4. What is the exact location of Shanghai?

_____

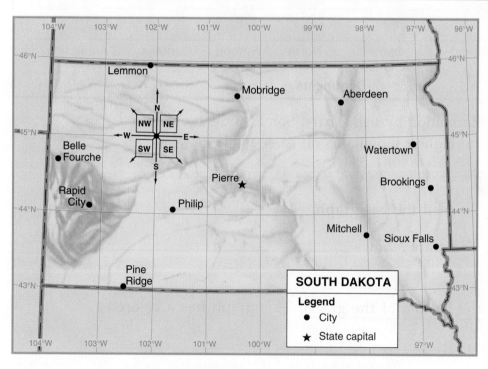

5. Which city in South Dakota is located near 44°N, 100°W?

_____

6. What three cities are located close to 102°W longitude?

_____

7. What is the exact location of Bell Fourche?

_____

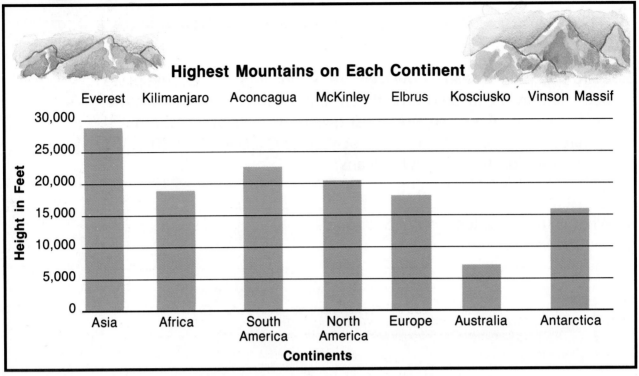

Highest Mountains on Each Continent

Bar graphs show information by using bars. Some students made a bar graph to compare the highest mountains on each continent.

GRAPH ATTACK!

Follow these steps to read the bar graph.

1. <u>Read the title.</u> This bar graph shows _____
_____.

2. <u>Read the words at the bottom of the graph.</u> This graph has a colored

   bar for each of seven _____.

3. <u>Read the words and numbers at the left of the graph.</u> The numbers on

   the graph stand for _____.

4. <u>Compare the bars.</u> Read the longest and shortest bars. Put your finger at the top of the bar for Mt. Everest. Slide your finger to the left. Read the number there.

   Mt. Everest is about _____ feet high.

   How high is Mt. Kosciusko? about _____ feet

5. <u>Draw a conclusion.</u> Which continents have the three highest mountains?

_____

Reading a Bar Graph

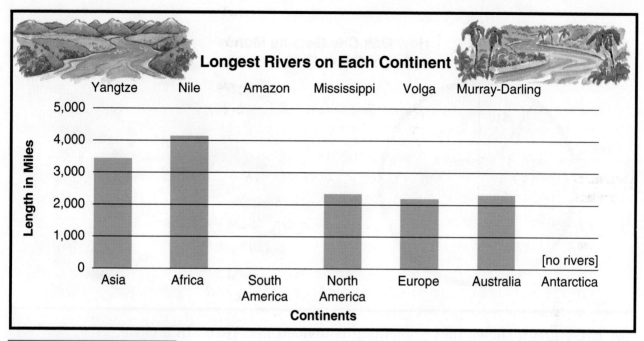

Longest Rivers on Each Continent

Yangtze   Nile   Amazon   Mississippi   Volga   Murray-Darling

Length in Miles: 5,000 / 4,000 / 3,000 / 2,000 / 1,000 / 0

[no rivers]

Asia   Africa   South America   North America   Europe   Australia   Antarctica

Continents

GRAPH ATTACK!

Follow these steps to read the bar graph.

1. <u>Read the title.</u> This bar graph shows _____

_____ .

2. <u>Read the words at the bottom of the graph.</u> The bars on this graph show

rivers on the _____ .

3. <u>Read the words and numbers at the left of the graph.</u> The numbers on

this graph stand for _____ .

4. <u>Add to the graph.</u> The Amazon River in South America is 4,000 miles long. Add a bar showing the length of the Amazon River.

5. <u>Compare the bars.</u> Read the longest and the shortest bars.

a. Which continent has the longest river? _____

b. About how long is it? _____

c. Which continent has the shortest river? _____

d. Which continent has no rivers? _____

6. <u>Draw a conclusion.</u> Which three continents have the longest rivers?

_____

Circle Graphs

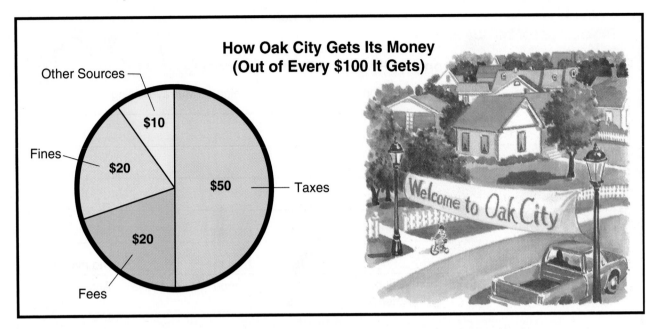

How Oak City Gets Its Money
(Out of Every $100 It Gets)

Other Sources

$10

Fines

$20

$50 — Taxes

$20

Fees

Welcome to Oak City

A **circle graph** shows how something is divided into parts. In a circle graph, the circle stands for the whole. Each part of the circle stands for a part of the whole.

GRAPH ATTACK!

Follow these steps to read the circle graph.

1. Read the title. The whole circle shows _____.

2. Read each part of the circle. What does each part of the circle stand for?

   _____

3. Read the biggest part of the circle. Oak City gets most of its money from

   _____. Out of every $100 it gets, $ ____ comes from this source.

4. Read the smallest part of the circle. Oak City gets the least amount of

   its money from _____. Out of every $100 it gets, $ ____
   comes from this source.

5. Compare the parts of the circle. Use <u>more</u> or <u>less</u> to complete each
   sentence.

   a. Oak City gets _____ of its money from fees than from taxes.

   b. Oak City gets _____ of its money from fines than from other sources.

6. Draw a conclusion. Which two sources are equal? _____

Reading a Circle Graph

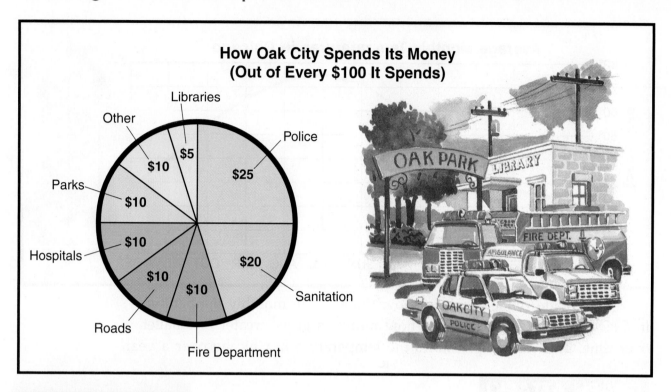

How Oak City Spends Its Money
(Out of Every $100 It Spends)

Libraries
Other
$5
$10
Police
$25
Parks
$10
$20
Hospitals
$10
Sanitation
Roads
$10
$10
Fire Department

GRAPH ATTACK!

Follow these steps to read the circle graph.

1. <u>Read the title.</u> This circle graph shows _____

_____.

2. <u>Read each part of the circle.</u> Out of every $100 Oak City spends, how

much does it spend on parks? _____

3. <u>Compare the parts of circle.</u> Use <u>more</u> or <u>less</u> in each sentence.

   a. Oak City spends _____ money on police than on roads.

   b. Oak City spends _____ money on hospitals than on sanitation.
   Use <u>largest</u> or <u>smallest</u> in each sentence.

   c. Oak City spends the _____ amount of money on libraries.

   d. Oak City spends the _____ amount of money on police.

4. <u>Draw a conclusion.</u> Look at the graph on page 66. Does Oak City have
   more ways to get money or more ways to spend money?

_____

Line Graphs

Average Monthly Temperatures in Chicago

A class made a line graph to show the average monthly temperatures in Chicago. A **line graph** shows how numbers grow greater or smaller over time. This line graph shows the temperature in Chicago over a year.

GRAPH ATTACK!

Follow these steps to read a line graph.

1. <u>Read the title.</u> This line graph shows _____.
2. <u>Read the words along the bottom of the graph.</u> This graph shows how

   the temperature changes between _____ and _____.
3. <u>Read the words and numbers on the left side of the graph.</u> These

   numbers stand for _____. The highest number is _____.
4. <u>Read the dots on the line.</u> Put your finger on the dot above January. Slide it to the left to read the temperature.

   In January the average temperature is _____.

   In April the average temperature is _____.
5. <u>Read the shape of the line.</u> Write <u>up</u> or <u>down</u> to complete each sentence.

   From January to July the temperatures go _____.

   From July to December the temperatures go _____.
6. <u>Draw a conclusion.</u> What are the three coldest months in Chicago?

   _____

Reading a Line Graph

Average Monthly Precipitation in Chicago

GRAPH ATTACK!

Follow the first three steps on page 68 to begin reading this line graph. **Precipitation** is rain and snow.

1. <u>Read the dots on the line.</u> Put your finger on the dot above January. Slide it to the left to read the amount of precipitation.

   In January there were _____ inches of precipitation.

   In April there were _____ inches of precipitation.

2. <u>Finish the graph.</u> Use the information below to add dots to the graph. Then connect the dots to finish the line.

   October 2.6 inches   November 2.3 inches   December 2.1 inches

3. <u>Read the shape of the line.</u> Write <u>up</u> or <u>down</u> to complete each sentence.

   From February to June the amount of precipitation goes _____.

   From September to February the amount of precipitation goes _____.
   The greatest change in precipitation is between what two months?

   _____

4. <u>Draw a conclusion.</u> Compare this graph with the one on page 68. Is there more precipitation in the coldest months or in the hottest months?

   _____

Time Lines

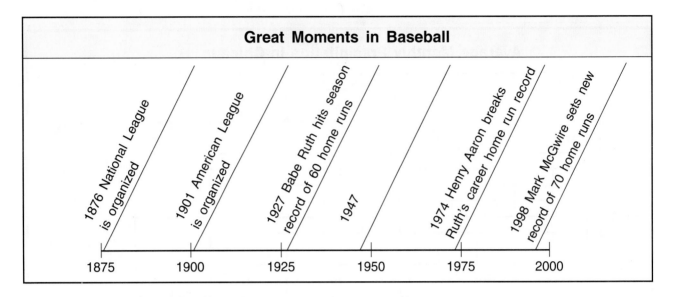

Great Moments in Baseball

1876 National League is organized

1901 American League is organized

1927 Babe Ruth hits season record of 60 home runs

1947

1974 Henry Aaron breaks Ruth's career home run record

1998 Mark McGwire sets new record of 70 home runs

1875   1900   1925   1950   1975   2000

A **time line** is a line that stands for a number of years. Marks on the line show the order in which events happened. They also show how far apart the events are in time. This time line shows great moments in the history of baseball.

TIME LINE ATTACK!

Follow these steps to read the time line.

1. Read the title. This time line shows _____.

_____

2. Read the dates along the bottom of the time line. This time line begins in

_____ and ends in _____.

3. Read the time line from left to right.

What happened in 1876? _____.

What happened in 1927? _____.

4. Add to the time line. In 1947, Jackie Robinson joined the Brooklyn Dodgers. Write "Jackie Robinson is first black major league player" on the line above 1947.

5. Study the order of events on the time line. Write before or after.

The American League was organized _____ the National League.

Jackie Robinson became the first black major league baseball player _____ Henry Aaron broke Babe Ruth's career home run record.

Reading a Time Line

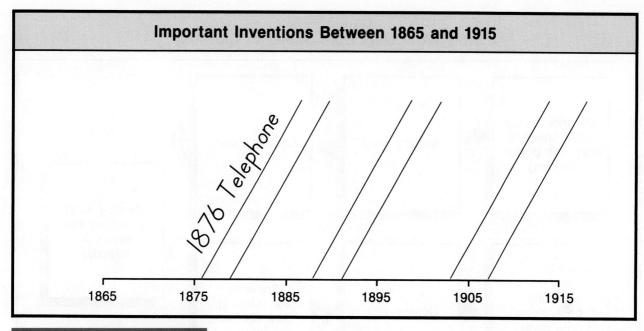

Important Inventions Between 1865 and 1915

1876 Telephone

1865   1875   1885   1895   1905   1915

TIME LINE ATTACK!

Follow the steps to read and finish this time line.

1. <u>Read the title.</u> This time line will show _____

   _____ .

2. <u>Read the dates along the bottom of the time line.</u> This time line

   begins in _____ and ends in _____ .

3. <u>Put the events in order.</u> Read the inventions below. Number them 1
   through 6 in the order they happened.

   _____ 1888 Camera   _____ 1891 Zipper

   _____ 1903 Airplane   _____ 1907 Helicopter

   _____ 1876 Telephone   _____ 1879 Lightbulb

4. <u>Write the events in order on the time line.</u> Write the events in order,
   from left to right on the time line. The first event is written for you.

5. <u>Study the order of events.</u> Write <u>before</u> or <u>after</u>.

   The telephone was invented _____ the zipper.

   The lightbulb was invented _____ the airplane.

   The helicopter was invented _____ the camera.

Flow Charts

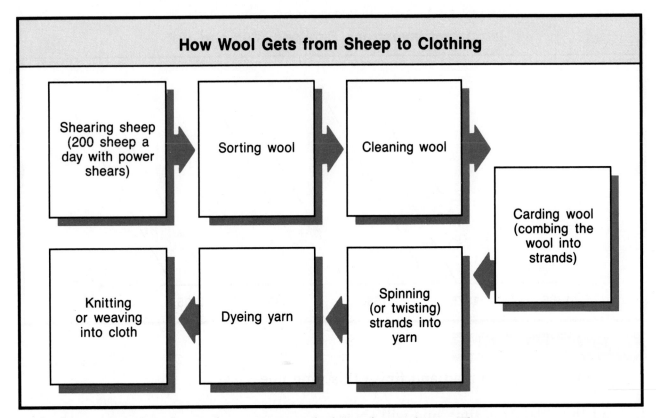

How Wool Gets from Sheep to Clothing

Shearing sheep (200 sheep a day with power shears) → Sorting wool → Cleaning wool → Carding wool (combing the wool into strands)

Knitting or weaving into cloth ← Dyeing yarn ← Spinning (or twisting) strands into yarn ← Carding wool

A class wanted to know how we get clothing from sheep. The teacher made a flow chart to show the steps from sheep to clothing. A **flow chart** is a drawing that shows the steps for doing or making something.

FLOW CHART ATTACK!

Follow these steps to read a flow chart.

1. <u>Read the title.</u> This flow chart shows the steps that explain

   _____ .

2. <u>Read the steps.</u> Follow the arrows. This flow chart starts at the top left corner. The first step in getting wool for clothing is

   _____ .

   The last step is _____ .

3. <u>Study the order of the steps.</u>

   Spinning or twisting takes places after _____ .

   Before the wool is carded, it has to be _____ and _____ .

Reading a Flow Chart

How We Get Baked Goods From Grain

1. Plant wheat seeds.

2. _____

3. Separate wheat berries from straw.

4. _____

5. At mill, grind berries into flour.

6. Haul flour to bakery.

7. _____

8. Bake bread, pretzels, cakes, and cookies.

FLOW CHART ATTACK!

Follow these steps to read and finish the flow chart.

1. Read the title. This flow chart shows how _____

   _____

   _____.

2. Read the steps. The first step is to _____.

   The last step is to _____.

3. Add these missing steps to the flow chart above.

   (2.) Harvest wheat.

   (4.) Haul wheat berries to mill for grinding.

   (7.) Make flour into dough.

4. Study the order of the steps.

   Before you haul wheat berries to the mill for grinding, you _____

   _____.

   After you grind berries into flour, you _____.

Geography Themes Up Close

Human/Environment Interaction describes how people adjust to their environment. In hot climates people wear light clothing. In cold, snowy climates, people build houses with slanted roofs so the snow slides off the roofs.

Human/Environment Interaction explains how people depend on the environment. They use natural resources to meet needs and wants. The maps below show land use and some products of Maine.

1. How do people use most of the land in southern Maine?

   _____

2. What industry developed along the coast of Maine?

   _____

3. Why would you expect the manufacturing of paper and wood products to be a leading industry in Maine?

   _____

   _____

Human/Environment Interaction explains how people change the environment. When people use the land and its resources to meet their needs, they change the environment. Some changes are good, but some cause problems.

4. Look at the photograph above. How have humans changed the environment? What could result from the changes?

_____

_____

_____

_____

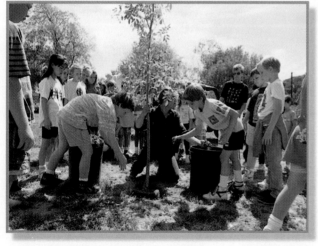

5. How are the people in this photograph trying to change the environment?

_____

_____

THE WORLD

0   1000   2000 MI

0   1000   2000   3000 KM

80°N

Arctic

60°N
Bering Sea

Hudson
Bay

NORTH

Great
Lakes

Rocky Mountains

40°N

Mississippi River

Appalachian Mountains

AMERICA

Atlantic Ocean

Tropic of Cancer

Gulf of
Mexico

20°N

Caribbean
Sea

Pacific Ocean

Andes

Equator

Amazon River

0°

SOUTH

AMERICA

Andes

20°S

Tropic of Capricorn

40°S

Andes

N
NW   NE
W   E
SW   SE
S

60°S

Antarctic Circle

80°S

180° 160°W 140°W 120°W 100°W 80°W 60°W 40°W 20°W
180° 160°W 140°W 120°W 100°W 80°W 60°W 40°W 20°W

Ocean

20°E 40°E 60°E 80°E 100°E 120°E 140°E 160°E 180°

80°N

Arctic Circle

Ural Mountains

ASIA

60°N

Volga River

EUROPE

Ob River

Alps

Danube River

Caspian Sea

40°N

Black Sea

Mediterranean Sea

The Himalaya

River

ntains

Ganges River

Red Sea

Arabian Sea

20°N

Pacific Ocean

AFRICA

Nile

Congo River

0°

Indian Ocean

20°S

AUSTRALIA

Great Dividing Range

40°S

60°S

ANTARCTICA

80°S

20°E 40°E 60°E 80°E 100°E 120°E 140°E 160°E 180°

THE UNITED STATES

- – – – – International Boundary
- – – – – State Boundary
- ⊛ National Capital
- ★ State Capital

500 MI
0   100   200   300   400   500

800 KM
0   100   200   300   400   500   600   700   800

CANADA

RUSSIA

Arctic Ocean

Alaska

CANADA

Juneau ★

Yukon River

400 MI
0   200   400

400 KM
0   200   400

Hawaii

Honolulu ★

100 MI
0   50   100

100 KM
0   50   100

Pacific Ocean

Atlantic Ocean

Gulf of Mexico

Pacific Ocean

MEXICO

N NE E
NW   SE
W   S
SW

Maine
Augusta ★

New Hampshire
Concord ★

Massachusetts
Boston ★

Vermont
Montpelier ★

Rhode Island
Providence ★

Connecticut
Hartford ★

New Jersey
Trenton ★

Delaware
Dover ★

Washington, D.C. ⊛
Maryland
Annapolis ★

New York
Albany ★

Lake Ontario

Lake Erie

Pennsylvania
Harrisburg ★

West Virginia
Charleston ★

Virginia
Richmond ★

North Carolina
Raleigh ★

South Carolina
Columbia ★

Ohio
Columbus ★

Kentucky
Frankfort ★

Tennessee
Nashville ★

Georgia
Atlanta ★

Alabama
Montgomery ★

Mississippi
Jackson ★

Florida
Tallahassee ★

Lake Okeechobee

Appalachian Mountains

Ohio River

Mississippi River

Indiana
Indianapolis ★

Illinois
Springfield ★

Michigan
Lansing ★

Lake Superior

Lake Huron

Lake Michigan

Wisconsin
Madison ★

Minnesota
St. Paul ★

Iowa
Des Moines ★

Missouri
Jefferson City ★

Arkansas
Little Rock ★

Louisiana
Baton Rouge ★

Oklahoma
Oklahoma City ★

Texas
Austin ★

Kansas
Topeka ★

Nebraska
Lincoln ★

South Dakota
Pierre ★

North Dakota
Bismarck ★

Red River

Minnesota River

Missouri River

Arkansas River

Red River

Brazos River

Rio Grande

New Mexico
Santa Fe ★

Colorado
Denver ★

Wyoming
Cheyenne ★

Montana
Helena ★

Idaho
Boise ★

Utah
Salt Lake City ★

Arizona
Phoenix ★

Nevada
Carson City ★

California
Sacramento ★

Oregon
Salem ★

Washington
Olympia ★

Rocky Mountains

Great Salt Lake

Colorado River

Snake River

Columbia River

Cascade Range

Sierra Nevada

Glossary

bar graph (p. 64)   a graph with thick lines, or bars, of different lengths to compare numbers or amounts

cardinal directions (p. 8)   north, south, east, and west

circle graph (p. 66)   a circle that shows how something whole is divided into parts

compass rose (p. 8)   a symbol that shows the cardinal and intermediate directions: north, northeast, east, southeast, south, southwest, west, and northwest

continent (p. 45)   a very large body of land

degrees (p. 51)   the unit of measurement used for lines of latitude and longitude

distance (p. 28)   how far one place is from another

Eastern Hemisphere (p. 57) the half of Earth east of the Prime Meridian

environment (p. 5)   the surroundings in which a person, animal, or plant lives

Equator (p. 50)   the imaginary line around the middle of Earth that divides Earth into the Northern and Southern Hemispheres

flow chart (p. 72)   a drawing that shows the steps for doing or making something

hemisphere (p. 50)   half the globe; half of Earth; the four hemispheres are Eastern, Western, Northern, and Southern

geography (p. 4)   the study of Earth and the ways people live and work on Earth

grid (p. 22)   a pattern of lines that cross each other to form squares

human features (pp. 4, 34)   features of a place or region made by people, such as buildings, roads, parks, playgrounds, bridges, railroads, farms, factories, and shopping malls

human/environment interaction (pp. 5, 74)   the ways people live with and change their environment

intermediate directions (p. 15)   northeast, southeast, southwest, northwest

interstate highway (p. 36)   a main highway that crosses the entire country

kilometers (p. 28)   a unit of length used in measuring distance in the metric system. Kilometers can also be written **KM** and km.

latitude (p. 51)   imaginary lines that circle Earth north and south of the Equator. They are numbered and marked by degrees. They are used to locate places.

legend (p. 9)   a map key, or list of symbols on a map and what they stand for

line graph (p. 68)   a graph that shows how something changes over time

location (pp. 4, 62)   where something on Earth is found

longitude (p. 56)   imaginary lines that go from the North Pole to the South Pole. They are numbered and marked by degrees. They are used to locate places.

map (p. 9)   a drawing of a real place that shows the place from above

map index (p. 23) the alphabetical list of places on a map with their grid squares

map key (p. 9) the guide that tells what the symbols on a map stand for

map scale (p. 28) the guide that tells what the distances on a map stand for

miles (p. 28) a unit of length used in measuring distance. Miles can also be written **MI** or mi.

mountain range (p. 43) a chain or group of mountains

movement (pp. 6, 20) how people, goods, information, and ideas move from place to place through transportation and communication

natural resources (p. 4) things in nature that people can use, such as water, trees, oil, and gold

Northern Hemisphere (p. 50) the half of Earth north of the Equator

physical features (pp. 4, 34) features of a place or region formed by nature, such as bodies of water, landforms, climate, natural resources, and plants and animals

place (pp. 4, 34) tells about the physical and human features of an area that make it different from other areas

plain (p. 43) a large area of flat land

precipitation (p. 69) rain and snow

Prime Meridian (p. 56) the line of longitude running from the South Pole to the North Pole and measured at 0°. It helps divide Earth into the Eastern and Western Hemispheres.

regions (pp. 7, 48) areas that share one or more features

relief map (p. 42) a map that shows elevation, or height, of land

resource (p. 10) things people can use. Some resources are oil, lumber, and water.

route (p. 36) a road or path from one place to another. Highways, railroads, waterways, and trails are routes.

Southern Hemisphere (p. 50) the half of Earth south of the Equator

state highway (p. 36) a main road that connects cities and towns within the boundaries of one state

symbol (p. 9) a picture on a map that stands for something real

time line (p. 70) a line that shows a number of years and the events that happened in order

title (p. 8) the name of a map, chart, or graph

U.S. highway (p. 36) a main highway that passes through more than one state

Western Hemisphere (p. 57) the half of Earth west of the Prime Meridian

Name _____

Use this map of famous tourist sights in Washington, D.C., to answer the questions.

SIGHTS IN WASHINGTON, D.C.

1. **The American History Museum, Natural History Museum, and National Gallery of Art are located on which side of the National Mall?**
   Ⓐ North
   Ⓑ East
   Ⓒ South
   Ⓓ West

2. **In which grid square do you find the Arts and Industries building?**
   Ⓐ C–3
   Ⓑ C–4
   Ⓒ D–2
   Ⓓ D–3

3. **What famous Washington sight is in grid square A–2?**
   Ⓐ The National Mall
   Ⓑ U.S. Capitol
   Ⓒ Washington Monument
   Ⓓ White House

4. **Which sight is farthest south?**
   Ⓐ African Art Museum
   Ⓑ American History Museum
   Ⓒ Smithsonian Castle
   Ⓓ Washington Monument

5. **Which direction would you travel to go from the White House to the U.S. Capitol?**
   Ⓐ Northeast
   Ⓑ Southeast
   Ⓒ Southwest
   Ⓓ Northwest

6. **Which museum is located in three different grid squares?**
   Ⓐ Air and Space Museum
   Ⓑ American History Museum
   Ⓒ Natural History Museum
   Ⓓ National Gallery of Art

Use this map of four imaginary states to answer the questions.

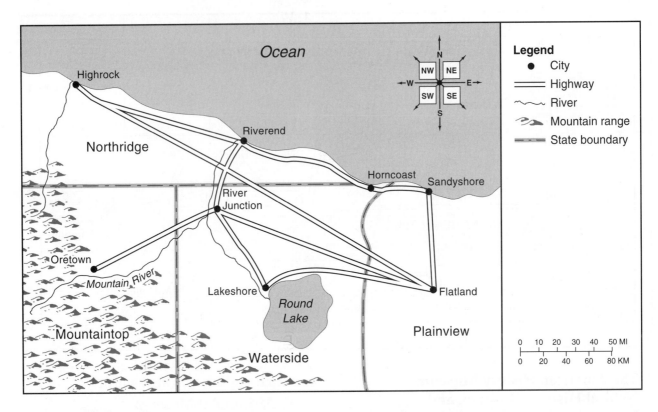

7. **On which trip would you cross the most states?**
   - Ⓐ Flatland to Lakeshore
   - Ⓑ Flatland to Highrock
   - Ⓒ Riverend to Highrock
   - Ⓓ Sandyshore to River Junction

8. **Which state has no rivers?**
   - Ⓐ Northridge
   - Ⓑ Mountaintop
   - Ⓒ Plainview
   - Ⓓ Waterside

9. **Which state has no mountains?**
   - Ⓐ Northridge
   - Ⓑ Mountaintop
   - Ⓒ Plainview
   - Ⓓ Waterside

10. **Where does Mountain River flow into the ocean?**
    - Ⓐ Highrock
    - Ⓑ Horncoast
    - Ⓒ Riverend
    - Ⓓ River Junction

11. **If you are traveling from Flatland to Sandyshore, about how many miles is the trip?**
    - Ⓐ 20
    - Ⓑ 50
    - Ⓒ 80
    - Ⓓ 100

12. **Highrock is located in which direction from Round Lake?**
    - Ⓐ Northeast
    - Ⓑ Southeast
    - Ⓒ Northwest
    - Ⓓ Southwest

Name _____

STANDARDIZED FINAL TEST

Use the route map below to answer the questions.

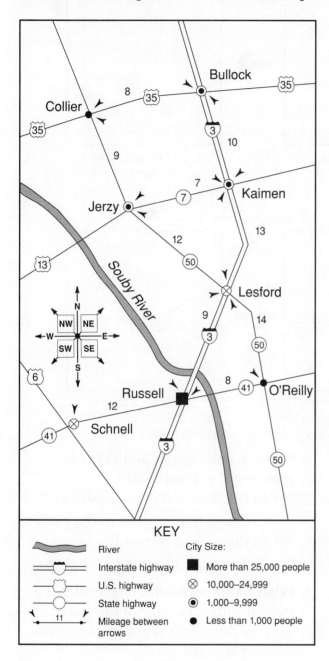

1. **Which highways do not cross the river?**
   Ⓐ 13 and 41
   Ⓑ 6 and 35
   Ⓒ 7 and 50
   Ⓓ 3 and 50

2. **What is the only interstate highway shown on the map?**
   Ⓐ 3
   Ⓑ 6
   Ⓒ 41
   Ⓓ 50

3. **In what general direction does State Highway 50 run?**
   Ⓐ North to south
   Ⓑ Northwest to east
   Ⓒ Northwest to southeast
   Ⓓ Southwest to northeast

4. **What is the shortest distance from Collier to Kaimen?**
   Ⓐ 9 miles
   Ⓑ 16 miles
   Ⓒ 18 miles
   Ⓓ 25 miles

5. **Which city is located 12 miles east and 9 miles northeast of Schnell?**
   Ⓐ Russell
   Ⓑ O'Reilly
   Ⓒ Lesford
   Ⓓ Kaimen

6. **What is the population of Jerzy?**
   Ⓐ Less than 1,000
   Ⓑ 1,000–9,999
   Ⓒ 10,000–24,999
   Ⓓ More than 25,000

Peanuts are taken out of their shells.

Peanuts are roasted. Then a machine removes the skins.

Peanuts are ground and mixed with sugar, oil, and salt.

Peanut butter is taken to stores to be sold.

Peanut butter is poured into jars. Lids and labels are put on the jars.

The mixture is stirred to make smooth, creamy peanut butter.

7. What would be a good title for this flow chart?
- Ⓐ The Harvesting of Peanuts
- Ⓑ How Peanuts are Prepared for Sale
- Ⓒ The Making of Peanut Butter
- Ⓓ The Preparation of Peanut Brittle

8. What do the six pictures shown here represent?
- Ⓐ The ingredients for making peanut butter
- Ⓑ Uses for peanuts
- Ⓒ Sources of peanuts for making peanut butter
- Ⓓ Steps for making peanut butter

9. If you were to number the steps shown in the flow chart, which step shows the mixing of ingredients?
- Ⓐ Step 2
- Ⓑ Step 3
- Ⓒ Step 4
- Ⓓ Step 5

10. When are the shells and skins removed from peanuts?
- Ⓐ In the first step of the process
- Ⓑ In two different steps of the process
- Ⓒ In the second step of the process
- Ⓓ Not enough information is given.

11. What happens immediately after the peanut butter in poured into jars?
- Ⓐ The mixture is stirred until creamy and smooth.
- Ⓑ The peanut butter is sold.
- Ⓒ The jars are taken to stores.
- Ⓓ Lids and labels are put on the jars.

12. If you were to number the steps shown in the flow chart, what would be a good label for Step 4?
- Ⓐ Mixing
- Ⓒ Pouring
- Ⓑ Stirring
- Ⓓ Labeling

Answer Key

Geography Introduction

Page 4 Location An address

Page 5 Place Question 1. Describe any three features of Baltimore, such as a river, skyscrapers, trees, sidewalks, and so on. **Question 2.** Describe three features of your town or city.
Human/Environment Interaction: Answers might include that in order to live near the ocean, people built their houses on pilings, or stilts to avoid floods or high tides from ocean water.

Page 6 Human/Environment Interaction
Answers will vary, but might include: to build houses or to farm and to connect land separated by water.

Page 7 Movement Information and ideas are moving through the computer.
Regions: Answers will vary, but might suggest that the Rocky Mountains form a region because of the obvious physical feature of the mountains or because of other physical features, such as the climate or animal life found in the Rocky Mountains.

1 • Directions and Legends

Page 8 Question 1. east **Question 2.** north

Page 9 Question 1. the funhouse, ticket booths, game booths, food stands, slide, mushroom ride, octopus ride, kiddie rides, and giraffe bounce **Question 2.** yes
Question 3. They are outside the scope of the map. **Question 4.** west **Question 5.** north
Question 6. south

Page 10 MAP ATTACK! Question 1.
Resources in Ohio **Question 2.** Each symbol should be checked. **Question 3.** North arrow on the compass rose should be circled; the other three arrows should be labeled correctly.
1.–3. Symbols should be circled to match directions. (corn, hay, sheep) **4.** Popcorn symbol should be added to the legend.
5. Popcorn symbols should be added in correct locations. **6.** salt **7.** popcorn

Page 11 1. brown **2.** Answer should fit your area. **3.** many **4.** many **5.** Answers will vary,

but may include the following: to find jobs, to live close to a large body of water.

Page 12 1. Maine **2.** Georgia **3.** Harrisburg
4. Potomac River **5.** Any two are correct: South Carolina, Delaware, New Jersey, or Rhode Island **6.** New York

Page 13 Word Check 1. map **2.** symbol
3. legend **4.** compass rose **5.** cardinal directions
Map Check 1. Hunger Mountain
2. Worcester **3.** Springfield **4.** Holyoke

2 • Intermediate Directions

Page 15 Question 1. Coliseum–southwest, Meigs Field–southeast, Sears Tower– northwest
Question 2. Union Station– southwest, Art Institute–southeast, Wrigley Building–northeast

Page 16 MAP ATTACK! Question 1. Illinois
Question 2. The compass rose arrows for the intermediate directions should be labeled correctly using the abbreviations.
1.–4. Lines should be drawn from Springfield to four cities. **1.** northeast **2.** southwest
3. southeast **4.** northwest

Page 17 MAP ATTACK! 1. a. Nebraska
b. Oklahoma or Texas **c.** Arizona **d.** Wyoming
2. a. SW **b.** NE **c.** NE **d.** SE **e.** NW **f.** SE **g.** NE
h. SE **i.** NE

Page 18 1.–3. Map should be colored to match directions. **4. b.** SE **c.** SW **d.** S **e.** N **f.** W **g.** SE
h. NW

Page 19 Word Check 1. Compass rose should be completed. **2.** Intermediate
Map Check 1. The island of Lanai should be circled on the map. **2.–4.** Lines should be drawn from Lanai to Maui, Hawaii, and Oahu. **2.** east **3.** southeast **4.** northwest
5. Mauna Loa, Mauna Kea

Geography Feature: Movement

Page 20 1. Railroad and highway
2. Albuquerque, because it has an airport, railroad, and major highway. **3.** route from Las Cruces to Santa Fe on Highway 25 traced on map; Highway 25

Page 20 **4.** Socorro, Albuquerque, Rio Rancho
Page 21 **5.** Answers will vary. **6.** 18 **7.** 41; more **8.** Answers will vary, but predictions should be greater than 41.

3 • Grids

Page 22 **Question 1.** bakery; B–2
Question 2. swimming pool; B–4
Question 3. north

Page 23 **Question 1.** D–1 **Question 2.** D–3
Question 3. B–2; State Capitol and State Railroad Museum **Question 4.** south

Page 24 **MAP ATTACK!** **Question 1.** Kansas
Question 2. The four intermediate directions should be correctly labeled on the compass rose. **Question 3.** 4; 8
1. Topeka **2.** Mt. Sunflower **3.** Wichita
4. Arkansas River **5.** Any two are correct: Garden City (C–2), Dodge City (D–3), or Wichita (D–5)

Page 25 **1.** Adding B–E down each side and 2–6 across the top and bottom of the map should complete the map grid. **2.** Each place should be circled. Mt. Rushmore–South Dakota; McCook– Nebraska; Cedar Rapids–Iowa; Grand Forks–North Dakota **3.** State capital names should be written on map. Jefferson City–Missouri; Pierre–South Dakota; Des Moines–Iowa; Lincoln–Nebraska; Topeka–Kansas

Page 26 **1.–2.** Seven places should be circled to match directions. **2.** Mammoth Hot Springs– NW; Amethyst Mountain–NE; Yellowstone Lake–S; Fountain Paintpots–SW; Bechler Ranger Station–SW **3.** Campground symbol should be drawn to match directions. **4.** Eagle Peak

Page 27 **Word Check 1.** index **2.** grid
Map Check 1. The map grid should be completed by adding B–D down each side and 2–7 across the top and bottom of the map. **2.** B–5; Mystery Mansion should be circled on the map. **3.** C–3; southwest **4.** C-7; southeast

4 • Distance and Scale

NOTE: All answers are approximate.

Page 28 **Question 1.** MI **Question 2.** KM

Page 29 210 miles (340 KM)

Page 30 **MAP ATTACK!** **Question 1.** The Denver Area **Question 2.** Each symbol should be checked. **Question 3.** The four intermediate direction arrows on the compass rose should be correctly labeled. **Question 4.** 3
1. 6 **2.** 8½ **3.** 4½ **4.** 7 **5.** 12

Page 31 **1.–5.** Lines should be drawn to match directions. **1.** about 225 **2.** about 140 **3.** about 85 **4.** about 105 **5.** about 555 (Should be the total of the answers for 1.–4.)

Page 32 **Day 2**–southwest; about 350
Day 3–southeast; about 230 **Day 4**–north; about 175 **Day 5**–northwest; about 350

Page 33 **Word Check 1.** miles, kilometers
2. map scale

Map Scale 1. 50 **2.** 80 **3.** 160 **4.** 85

Geography Feature: Place

Page 34 **1.** Rock Creek Park should be labeled on the map. **2.** Potomac River, Anacostia River **3.** The Capitol should be circled and marked with H on the map. **4.** Any two of the following: National Zoological Park, Walter Reed Army Medical Center, Catholic University of America, American University, U.S. Naval Observatory, Howard University, Union Station, Jefferson Memorial, Washington Monument, Lincoln Memorial, White House

Page 35 **5.** Colorado River should be labeled and marked with P on the map. **6.** Any two of the following: Rampart Cave, Kanab Plateau, Coconino Plateau, Kaibab Plateau, Shivwits Plateau, Point Imperial, North Rim, South Rim, Granite Rapids, canyons, Kanab Creek **7.** Grand Canyon Village should be circled on the map. **8.** Any two of the following: roads, hiking trail, populated places **9.** Answers will vary, but may point out that Washington, D.C., has more human features, but the Grand Canyon has more physical features.

5 • Route Maps

Page 36 **Question 1.** 5, 15, 35, 95
Question 2. 90, 40, 10 **Question 3.** 20, 93, 83, 82 **Question 4.** 33 (CA), 23 (MN), 114 (TX), 17 (NY), 20 (FL)

Page 37 **Question 1.** 59 **Question 2.** 130
Question 3. 114 **Question 4.** 32 **Question 5.** 101
Question 6. 71 **Question 7.** 204

Page 38 **MAP ATTACK!** **Question 1.** routes in central Mississippi **Question 2.** interstate highway, U.S. highway, and state highway **Question 3.** The four intermediate direction arrows on the compass rose should be correctly labeled.
1. Interstate 20 **2.** U.S. 61 **3.** U.S. 49 **4.** Yazoo City and Tchula **5.** Carthage should be added to the map. **6.** U.S. 51

Page 39 **1.** Routes in Texas **2.** Austin to San Antonio–72; Laredo to Brownsville–200; Amarillo to Lubbock–122; Abilene to Fort Worth–150; Dallas to Houston–237; San Antonio to Corpus Christi–133 **3.** Corpus Christi to Dallas–415; El Paso to Fort Worth–598; Abilene to Brownsville–572; San Antonio to El Paso–558

Page 40 **MAP ATTACK!** **1.** Key West to Long Key–65; Jupiter to Boca Raton–45; Ft. Lauderdale to Miami Beach–22 **2.** 100 **3.** Key Largo **4.** 239

Page 41 **Word Check 1.** interstate highway **2.** state highway **3.** U.S. highway **4.** route
Map Check 1. Interstate 82 **2.** Olympia, Tacoma, Seattle, and Bellingham **3.** U.S. 101 **4.** 20

6 • Relief Maps

Page 42 **Question 1.** Medicine Mountains; They have darker shading. **Question 2.** Pancake Valley; It has no shading.

Page 43 **Question 1.** the Rocky Mountains **Question 2.** Cascade Range–northwest coast; Sierra Nevada–west of Great Salt Lake; Rocky Mountains–west of Great Plains;

Appalachian Mountains–near the east coast **Question 3.** Rocky Mountains; They have darker shading. **Question 4.** western **Question 5.** Rocky Mountains

Page 44 **MAP ATTACK!** **Question 1.** a relief map of Alaska **Question 2.** Each symbol should be checked. **Question 3.** The four intermediate direction arrows on the compass rose should be circled.
1. Labels should be added to show three mountain ranges and Mt. McKinley. **2.** Yukon River **3.** a valley

Page 45 **1.** Labels for all mountain ranges should be circled. **2.** North America–Rocky Mountains or Appalachian Mountains; South America–Andes; Europe–Alps or Ural Mountains; Asia–Ural Mountains or The Himalaya; Africa–Atlas Mountains

Page 46 **1.** Interstate 5 should be traced in red.; Cascade Range and Sierra Nevada **2.** 1,400 **3.** The Rocky Mountains should be colored green.; Interstate 15 **4.** Cheyenne, Wyoming, should be circled. **5.** Interstate 80 from Cheyenne to Sacramento should be traced. **6.** Rocky Mountains and Sierra Nevada

Page 47 **Word Check 1.** relief map **2.** mountain range **3.** plain
Map Check 1. Labels should be added to show the two mountain ranges and Mt. Mitchell. **2.** west

Geography Feature: Regions

Page 49 **1.** Human feature—speech **2.** Western region **3.** Answers will vary, depending on your location. **4.** New England region **5.** Illinois, Indiana, Ohio, Pennsylvania, West Virginia, and New Jersey **6.** Answers will vary but might point out that transportation and communication have brought people closer together. There is more contact with people who might speak differently. For example, television allows people in all parts of the United States to hear the way most people pronounce words. As a result, people are beginning to have common pronunciations.

7 • Latitude

Page 50 South America, Africa, Pacific Ocean, Atlantic Ocean, Indian Ocean

Page 51 Question 1. North America, Europe, Asia **Question 2.** Australia

Page 52 1. The Equator should be traced in red on the map. Quito **2.** 20°N should be traced in green on the map. Mexico City **3.** 20°S should be traced in orange on the map. Sucre **4.** 40°N should be traced in yellow on the map. Denver **5.** Houston should be circled in green on the map. 30°N **6.** Lima should be circled in red on the map. 10°S

Page 53 1. Quito **2.** Potosí **3.** Caracas **4.** Valdivia **5.** Paramaribo, 5°N **6.** Asunción, 25°S **7.** Buenos Aires, 34°S or 35°S

Page 54 1. Pôrto Alegre, Brisbane **2.** Guatemala City, Manila **3.** Cairo **4.** Vancouver **5.** Oslo **6.** Quito **7.** Lusaka **5.** Antarctica **9.** NE **10.** SW **11.** NW

Page 55 Word Check 1. Equator **2.** latitude **3.** Northern Hemisphere **4.** Southern Hemisphere **5.** degrees
Map Check 1. Manta **2.** Esmeraldas **3.** Loja **4.** Guayaquil **5.** Cuenca

8 • Longitude

Page 56 Question 1. Europe, Africa, Antarctica **Question 2.** Arctic Ocean, Atlantic Ocean

Page 57 Question 1. Africa, Antarctica **Question 2.** Arctic Ocean, Atlantic Ocean **Question 3.** Europe, Asia, Africa, Antarctica

Page 58 1. The Prime Meridian should be traced in red on the map. London **2.** 5°W should be traced in green on the map. Glasgow **3.** 5°E should be traced in orange on the map. Lyon **4.** 10°E should be traced in yellow on the map. Hamburg **5.** 10°W should be traced in purple on the map. Lisbon **6.** 15°E should be traced in brown on the map. Salerno

Page 59 1. London **2.** Tunis **3.** Lisbon **4.** Cape Town **5.** Cairo **6.** Vologda **7.** Tehran

Page 60 1. St. Petersburg, Alexandria **2.** Denver **3.** Manila **4.** Canberra **5.** Bogotá **6.** Greenwich **7.** SE **8.** NE

Page 61 Word Check 1. longitude **2.** Prime Meridian **3.** Eastern Hemisphere **4.** Western Hemisphere
Map Check 1. Birmingham **2.** London **3.** Belfast **4.** Glasgow **5.** Clifden

Geography Feature: Location

Page 62 1. Answers will vary but might say that North America is north of South America, west of the Atlantic Ocean, and east of the Pacific Ocean. **2.** Cairo and New Orleans should be circled on the map.

Page 63 3. 30°N, 90°W **4.** 30°N, 120°E **5.** Pierre **6.** Lemmon, Philip, Pine Ridge **7.** 45°N, 104°W

9 • Graphs

Page 64 1. the highest mountains on each continent **2.** continents **3.** height in feet **4.** 29,000; 7,000 **5.** Asia, South America, and North America

Page 65 1. the longest rivers on each continent **2.** continents **3.** length in miles **4.** A bar should be added to the graph for the Amazon River in South America for 4,000 miles. **5. a.** Africa **b.** about 4,100 miles long **c.** Europe **d.** Antarctica **6.** Asia, Africa, and South America

Page 66 1. how Oak City gets its money **2.** amount of money from taxes, fees, fines, and other sources **3.** taxes; 50 **4.** other sources; 10 **5. a.** less **b.** more **6.** fees and fines

Page 67 1. how Oak City spends its money **2.** $10 **3. a.** more **b.** less **c.** smallest **d.** largest **4.** It has more ways to spend money.

Page 68 1. average monthly temperatures in Chicago **2.** January, December **3.** temperature; 80° **4.** 24° to 26°; 50° **5.** up; down **6.** The three coldest months are January, February, and December.

Page 69 1. 1.9; **3.** 1 **2.** The graph should be completed to match directions, **3.** up; down; February and March **4.** There is more precipitation in the hottest months.

Page 70 1. Great moments in baseball **2.** 1875; 2000 **3.** National League was organized.; Babe Ruth hit a season record 60 home runs. **4.** "Jackie Robinson is first black major league player" should be added to time line above 1947. **5.** after; before

Page 71 1. important inventions between 1865 and 1915 **2.** 1865; 1915 **3.** 1888 Camera–3; 1903 Airplane–5; 1876 Telephone–1; 1891 Zipper–4; 1907 Helicopter–6; 1879 Lightbulb–2 **4.** The time line should be completed by adding dates and labels for five events. **5.** before; before; after

Page 72 1. how wool gets from sheep to clothing **2.** shearing sheep; knitting or weaving into cloth **3.** carding wool; sorted, cleaned

Page 73 1. we get baked goods from grain **2.** plant wheat seeds; bake bread, pretzels, cakes, and cookies **3.** The chart should be completed to match directions. **4.** separate wheat berries from straw; haul flour to bakery

Geography Feature:
Human/Environment Interaction

Page 74 1. for farming **2.** fishing **3.** Answers will vary, but might explain that Maine has many forests and that paper and wood products are made from trees.

Page 75 4. Humans damaged the environment by destroying the forest. Answers will vary, but might suggest that habitats are destroyed for many plants and animals. Also, because the trees have been cut down, there is nothing to hold the soil in place and erosion can occur. **5.** They are trying to save and protect the environment by planting trees that can hold the soil in place and be homes for some kinds of wildlife.

Sample Standardized Test • Book 1

Page 81 1. A **2.** D **3.** C **4.** A **5.** B **6.** D

Page 82 7. B **8.** C **9.** C **10.** C **11.** B **12.** C

Page 83 1. C **2.** A **3.** C **4.** B **5.** C **6.** B

Page 84 7. C **8.** D **9.** B **10.** B **11.** D **12.** B

THE UNITED STATES

Maps•Globes•Graphs Book 1 © 2000 Steck-Vaughn Company

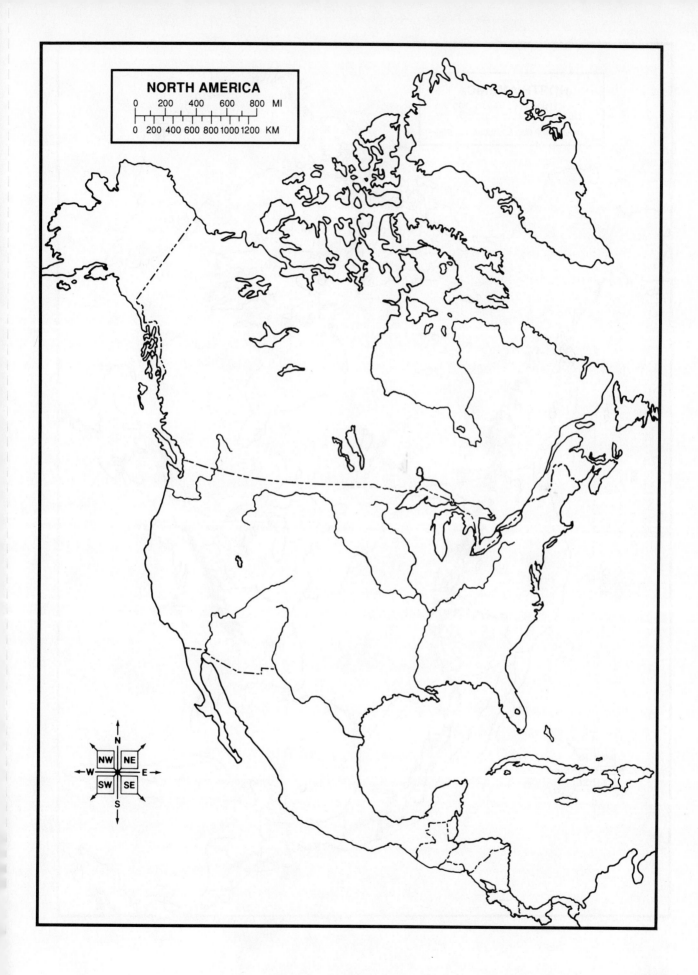

NORTH AMERICA

0   200   400   600   800 MI

0 200 400 600 800 1000 1200 KM

N
NW | NE
W   E
SW | SE
S

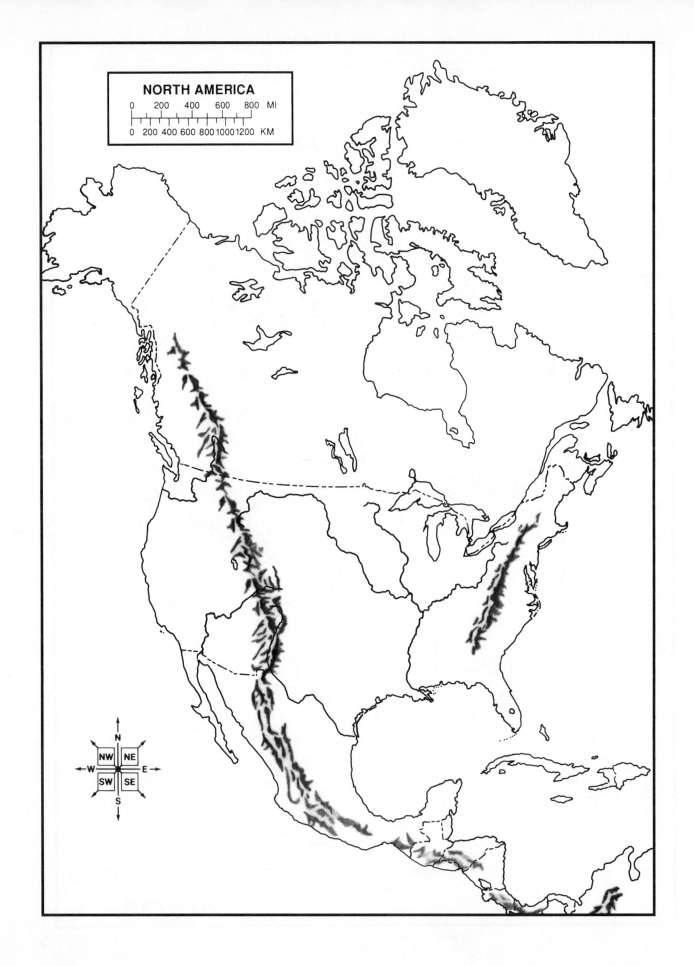

NORTH AMERICA

0   200   400   600   800   MI

0 200 400 600 800 1000 1200 KM

N
NW | NE
W ← | → E
SW | SE
S

Maps•Globes•Graphs   Book 1   © 2000 Steck-Vaughn Company

EASTERN HEMISPHERE

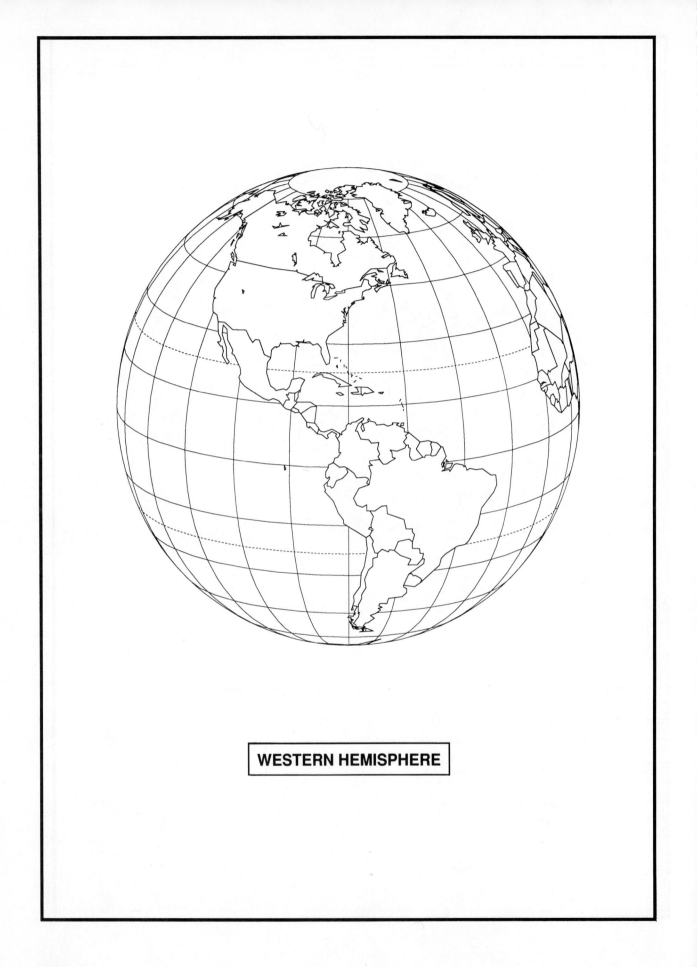

WESTERN HEMISPHERE

Maps•Globes•Graphs Book 1 © 2000 Steck-Vaughn Company

THE WORLD

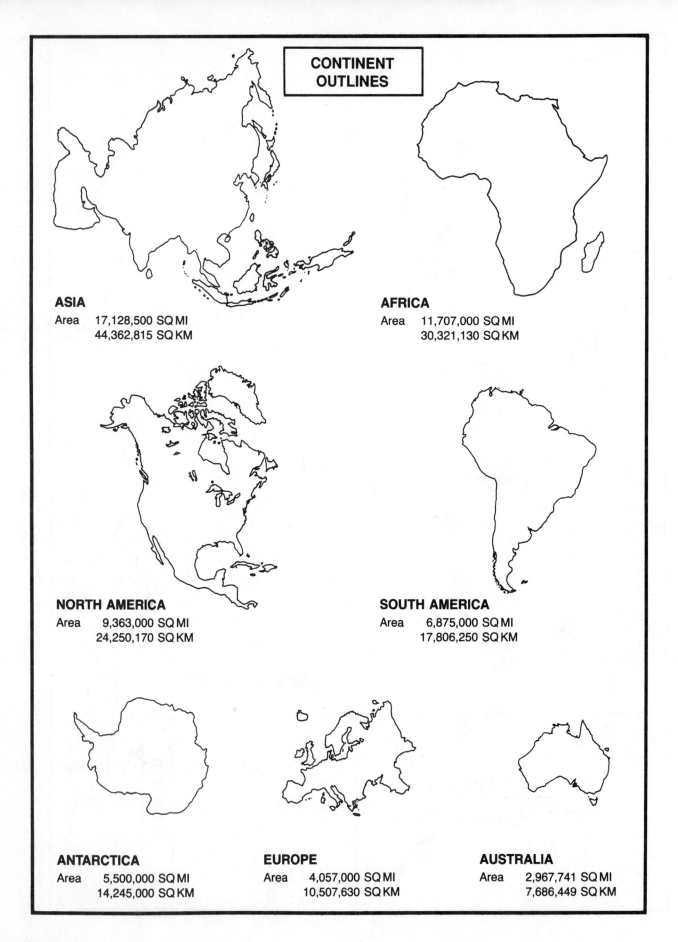

CONTINENT OUTLINES

ASIA
Area   17,128,500 SQ MI
        44,362,815 SQ KM

AFRICA
Area   11,707,000 SQ MI
        30,321,130 SQ KM

NORTH AMERICA
Area   9,363,000 SQ MI
        24,250,170 SQ KM

SOUTH AMERICA
Area   6,875,000 SQ MI
        17,806,250 SQ KM

ANTARCTICA
Area   5,500,000 SQ MI
        14,245,000 SQ KM

EUROPE
Area   4,057,000 SQ MI
        10,507,630 SQ KM

AUSTRALIA
Area   2,967,741 SQ MI
        7,686,449 SQ KM

Maps•Globes•Graphs Book 1 © 2000 Steck-Vaughn Company